ENDINGS

A BOOK FOR ALMOST EVERYONE

*To dear Lesley,
with warm wishes*

BETTY JANE WYLIE

Betty Jane Wylie

Cover artwork © *Theo Dimson 1982*
Author illustration © *Heather Spears*

tellwell

Tellwell Talent
www.tellwell.ca

ISBN
978-0-2288-0879-4 (Hardcover)
978-0-2288-0878-7 (Paperback)
978-0-2288-0880-0 (eBook)

By the same author

NON-FICTION

Letters to Icelanders: Exploring the Northern Soul

Enough: Lifestyle and Financial Planning for Simpler Living

Family: An Exploration

Beginnings: A Book for Widows

The Best Is Yet to Come

Life's Losses (later edition of New Beginnings)

Everywoman's Moneybook (with Lynne Macfarlane)

New Beginnings: Living Through Loss and Grief

All in the Family: A Survival Guide for Living and Loving in a Changing World

Successfully Single

COOKBOOKS

Solo Chef: Recipes, Tips, Advice and Encouragement for Single Cooks

The Betty Jane Wylie Cheese Cookbook

Encore: The Leftovers Cookbook

POETRY

The Better Half: Women's Voices

Something Might Happen

The Second Shepherds' Play (one version)

BELLES LETTRES

Reading Between the Lines: The Diaries of Women

Men! A Collection of Quotations About Men by Women

BIOGRAPHY

The Book of Matthew

The Horsburgh Scandal (play as well)

INSPIRATIONAL

Betty Jane's Diary: Lessons Children Taught Me

Betty Jane's Diary: Passages

Betty Jane's Diary: Holidays and Celebrations

No Two Alike

CHILDREN'S BOOKS

John of a Thousand Faces

Tecumseh

PLAYS

Veranda

Time Bomb

Double Vision

The Horsburgh Scandal (with Theatre Passe Muraille)

Moon and Murna

Jason

Androgyne

Angel

Speculum

Grace Under Pressure

The Second Shepherds' Play (2 translations, 1 adaptation; Musical)

Steps

How to Speak Male

Help is on the Way (six-part series)

A Day In the Life (two short plays, one theme)

A Place on Earth (one-hander)

Double Swap (with Michael Cole)

Size Ten

I See You

An Enemy of the People (adaptation)

PLAYS FOR CHILDREN

Don't Just Stand There - Jiggle! (5 puppet plays)

Kingsayer

The Old Woman and the Pedlar

ACKNOWLEDGEMENTS ix
DEDICATION xi
PREFACE...xiii

ACKNOWLEDGEMENTS

I am beholden to Jennifer Penney, my computer angel, without whom this book would not exist physically, nor I, emotionally.

My heartfelt devotion and thanks to Richard Teleky, my nag and mentor, and his dog, Toby, who keep me challenged and comforted, in that order.

For separate assistance and information, Susan Girvan and Susan Sutherland deserve my gratitude for services rendered.

To Marla Hayes, formerly my pupil, now my peer, guide and inspiration, goes my humble acknowledgement of a daily debt.

William Wolfe-Wylie, my grandson and techie guru, has earned my awe and recognition of his superior skill and his generosity withal.

And Marianne Brandis, my role model, though she is (a little) younger than I am, merits my attention and appreciation.

Equally important to me in the writing of this book were two grants, one from the Wallace Stegner Foundation, comprising one month (October) free residency in Stegner House in Eastend, Saskatchewan, with a $500 stipend, and a travel grant from the Canada Council for the Arts to help me get there (I live in Toronto, Ontario). I went by train so I could carry all my papers and research with me. The trip was valuable, too, because it afforded me a decompression chamber (2 days and 2 nights) to think and prepare for a demanding work schedule. I wrote my first draft of *Endings* in Stegner House and I am very grateful for the time and space granted to me.

My thanks to Nicole Dimson for the use of a poster design by her father, the artist Theo Dimson, for the cover of this book, and to Heather Spears, artist, for the use of her ageless drawing of me many years ago.

And *Wikipedia*.

DEDICATION

To Bill

PREFACE

My husband died suddenly 46 years ago after 20 years of marriage. We had four children, still unfinished, still in the midst of growing up, as I was, in the midst of a life now irrevocably changed.

I had been a stay-at-home mother with a difference. I was a writer, and I worked at it; that is, when I didn't have dinners or birthday parties, or flu or mumps or vacations or special events to cope with. I was a playwright with some claim to the title, having had several plays produced in Winnipeg, Stratford and Toronto, but I had never had to make a living at my vocation. Now I did.

There's a saying attributed to the Canadian playwright Bernard Slade (1930–2017) that "you can make a killing in the theatre, but you can't make a living." I knew that. What I didn't know is that you can't make a living as a writer, either, unless your name is headline-famous. I decided to hang out my shingle as a writer, a journalist, and try to leave enough spare time and energy to keep on writing plays.[1] That way, I could still be a stay-at-home mother and look after my youngest child, who is challenged. Oddly enough, I managed to do this, which I recount in my book *The Right Track: How to Succeed as a Freelance Writer in Canada* (1998).

My first book grew out of an article on my widowhood that appeared in *MacLean's* magazine.[2] That evolved into a commissioned series for the Canadian Life and Health Insurance Association and then segued into a book, *Beginnings: A Book for Widows* (1977). It went through several printings each of 4 or 5 editions, plus 2

---

[1] Can you believe that I was this naïve?
[2] It had the largest influx of fan letters to date. I did, too.

xiii

printings in the U.S. and big print in the U.K. It remained in print for 27 years and developed a devoted cult following of absolutely powerless women who lend each other my book.[3]

I was the darling of the insurance industry, casting myself as a professional widow, young enough to be a prime example of how not to back into widowhood. London Life Insurance Company used to give a copy of the book with every death claim they settled, and they had a wailing wall at their head office where they posted their thank-you letters—no wails, only praise and thanks. Most (Protestant) churches kept a copy in their libraries, and a lot of funeral associations did too. Whenever and wherever I spoke, and no matter the subject (frequently playwriting, or whatever my latest book was about), there would inevitably be two women in the audience who came up after to touch me (!) and tell me, "You saved my life."

Now that the book is out of print and my friends have reached the age when their husbands are dying, I buy copies of it from secondhand bookstores via Amazon to offer help. It was the book I needed and couldn't find when my husband died, and it continues to be helpful for others.

Now you understand why I have titled this book *Endings*, and I dedicate it to all the women (mainly) who have grown old with me, plus all the younger ones, men, too, the Boomers who scarcely know how to deal with death, to say nothing of its not always prerequisite corollary: age.

What we call the beginning is often the end
And to make an end is to make a beginning.
The end is where we start from.

-T.S. Eliot (1888-1965)

---

[3]   Though I have published more than 30 books, plays, poetry, musicals, etc., there is only one book to these fans.

Table of Contents

INTRODUCING: THIS OLD WOMAN.............................1

Chapter 1: COUNTING.......................................11

Chapter 2: NEEDING...19

Chapter 3: DOWNSIZING 25

Chapter 4: HITTING THE ROAD.......................37

Chapter 5: AGING 45

Chapter 6: MOVING ON..................................57

Chapter 7: SEARCHING FOR SELF..................63

Chapter 8: REMEMBERING 71

Chapter 9: FORGETTING 81

Chapter 10: CAREGIVING................................91

Chapter 11: TAKING COMFORT 101

Chapter 12: CHOOSING 109

Chapter 13: GOING SOLO 117

Chapter 14: FINDING SELF 123

Chapter 15: DISCOVERING..............................131

Chapter 16: BEING NICE 139

Chapter 17: LEAVING 149

EPILOGUE: THIS WOMAN, OLDER...........................155

APPENDIX 161

BIBLIOGRAPHY for *ENDINGS*...........................167

THIS OLD WOMAN

Well, I get tired. And when I say tired, it's like all the water running out of a bathtub and there's nothing left, not a drop. But my will has always been stronger than my flesh so I can force myself to meet an occasion. After the occasion, however, I am empty and dried up for about 24 hours until I can refill the tub.

The Austrian-Canadian endocrinologist Hans Selye (1907-1982) was the first person I was aware of who analyzed stress and how much of it we could manage. He used the image of a well instead of a bathtub, and his theory, as I understand it, was that you have only so much water (energy, resilience) in the well. When you use a lot of it, you have to allow time for it to refill but it never quite recovers its full capacity, and I suppose in time it drains completely. So my well is shallower than it was. However, I was fortunate to have quite a deep one to begin with.

Fortunate, too, that I don't take pills, just calcium, a daily vitamin for women over 50, and Vitamin D because I live in a cold, dark part of this continent, deprived of sunshine for a major part of the year. I take a lot, tonnes, in fact (that's a metric quantity, because I'm Canadian). I wonder if it's possible to OD on D. Anyway, no medications, no prescription drugs, no therapy, just DIY exercise and good food I prepare for myself. (I have published three cookbooks: one about leftovers, another on cheese and a third about cooking for one.) I swim for half an hour every morning at 6. My apartment building has an indoor and outdoor pool and an exercise room with various instruments designed to improve one's breathing and to create good muscles and a clear conscience. I prefer to ride a recumbent machine that leaves my hands free to hold a book, usually a mystery, so that I can read while I pedal to stay ahead of boredom. I try to keep my appointment with a thriller for half an hour every afternoon but life often interferes: guests or an early theatre or class— I was also taking Icelandic, a difficult language that rendered me very humble.

A dozen years ago now my cataracts ripened (love that word), and I acquired lenses that enabled me to see distances without a prescription for the first time since I was 13 years old. About 2 years ago, the lenses clouded over, and I couldn't see very well, near or far. I was granted a consult and experts agreed I couldn't see much. I said I knew that and I wanted them to do something. They resisted; it was only a consult. I resisted, too. I usually don't do this. I don't complain; I don't argue; I'm nice. I've always been very meek and mild, as befits a woman of my age and class. But my eyes are my tools, my source of income and joy. I told them that I had to be able to read and write. I said I wouldn't leave until something was done. So they scraped my lenses. I hate the thought, the image it conjures up of scraping, scratching and rasping, but the procedure was effective and I could see to work again. So here I am, sighted. I use magnifying spectacles and keep them all over the house to read recipes and letters, and I also wear prescription glasses for reading, not much different from the magnifying ones, except they have designer frames and they cost more.

The neat thing about wonky eyes is that you can play games with them. I remember a piece by the American writer James Thurber (1894–1961), whose eyes were damaged in a childhood accident that rendered him almost blind in later life. He described a big, patient dog he liked to watch from his office window. The dog wasn't on the ground; it lay above the front door, on the lintel, very still and very patient. Thurber loved the dog and admired its patience and loyalty. Later, when he got new, stronger glasses, he stopped looking out that window. He never wanted to find out what the dog really was. That's what I remember of the story. I have kept my use of it, and the justification it gives me to play around with what I think I see. I do have to be careful, though.

The lenses have endowed me with stereoptical vision. If I tilt my head at a certain angle, I see two images, and I have to re-tilt to make them blend into one, not three-dimensional, of course. That's kind of fun except when I negotiate escalator and subway stairs and have to focus clearly. I do like to land on the right step. As Penelope Lively (b. 1933) said in her memoir, *Dancing Fish and Ammonites* (2013), "Stay vertical if you possibly can."

I don't need a cane, and I am certainly not in the market for a walker but, like a writer friend of mine, I am grateful for banisters. He says he has reached the age when "banisters are not merely ornamentation." Whatever else I may forget, I never forget a good line and its source.

Anyway, good lines are easy. Faces are hard. Like the late neurologist and author, Oliver Sacks (1933–2015), I suffer from prosopagnosia, face blindness—the inability to remember faces. I also have no sense of direction. Neither of these handicaps has anything to do with my age; I've been like this all my life. I do have a good sense of time, though. I like to say I lost my map when I was born, but I swallowed a clock. There are GPS devices available to help the directionally challenged. So far, there's no GPS available to map faces, though I understand that facial recognition is coming. Better to be friendly to strangers than to ignore people I know who know me and who know I know them. The older I get, the more I am forgiven. That's a blessing.

I've been compiling a list of things I like about getting old(er). I gave up my car several years ago, before it was taken forcibly from me. I'll tell you why I relinquished it if you'll forgive me sounding noble. I wanted to reduce my footprint on the planet. Truly. A car leaves a big footprint. It also costs a lot of money, which honestly hadn't occurred to me. My dog died so I didn't need the car, so then the car went, too, and I couldn't believe how much money I had (for a while), like, ready cash. So I guess that's one of the things I appreciate, but I mention it because of what else the lack of a car gave me: the efficient, costly, crowded and cosmopolitan public transit system of Toronto (TTC). What a revelation! Among the most striking of my discoveries are the people who stand up for old people—primarily young Asian women, then young black men— at least, on the Toronto subway. I murmur my thanks as I sink gratefully onto a seat, adding, "It's nice to be old." Here are a few other nice things about old age:

MY TOP TEN NICE THINGS ABOUT BEING OLD

10. I don't have to stand on public transit.
9. I don't have to shave my legs.
8. I don't hemorrhage once a month. I still appreciate that.
7. I don't fuss about dust. I just take off my glasses.
6. I can take a nap when I feel like it.
5. I brag about my age.
4. I have forgiven almost everybody.
3. I still have my marbles, give or take.
2. I like me.
1. I'm still here.

I'm 88, and I feel fine. The American architect Buckminster Fuller (1895–1983) said that means you feel nothing, that is, nothing hurts. Katherine Hepburn (1907–2003) said there's only one answer to anyone who asks you how you feel: The answer is "fine," and if that makes you think of *The Philadelphia Story*, the play by Philip Barry (1896–1949), on which the film was based, then you must be about my age.

I get tired, did I mention that? Especially when I walk a lot. How much is a lot? Less than it used to be,[4] and you'd have to pace yourself to gear down to my speed. I have fallen several times but haven't broken anything yet.

Flash! I am editing this book now with one finger of my right hand because one week after I turned 88 I fell on ice and broke my left wrist. People think that's okay because I'm right-handed, but one needs the opposable left. I didn't expect a comeuppance like this. Keeps me humble. I discovered that I am not invincible, and I am chastened by the fact.

I still bounce. Mind you, bouncing can hurt. When it did, I kept swimming but took the time to stick the aching rib or limb, neck or shoulder, into a jet of the hot tub, and sigh (or groan) in gratitude. This one is going to take longer.

The non-physical symptoms of age are subtler and are often a matter of time. Once it took me two days to remember the name for walrus ivory carving (scrimshaw). I think that was my record. If a name or a word is slow to surface, I blame it on my inner Rolodex file. It's just getting a little rusty, or else it's overloaded. People with apps don't have this problem, but I don't have apps. I am not a Luddite. I have a desktop computer, a small laptop and a mini tablet. No Facebook, though, no Twitter or tweets, no Instagram or Pinterest, no Listings or #hashtags. I do have a website, and I write a daily blog, also a daily diary. I know it sounds like double-entry bookkeeping, but I write different things in each. No cell phone, at least until recently.

After my recent fall, my family insisted I get a cell phone so that I could ask for help. I have always relied on the kindness of strangers. So I bought a senior phone, with big numbers for blunt

---

4   I have osteoporosis, but I try to ignore it. My bone density is improving.

fingers and magnified eyes to negotiate and an SOS button. Now I must remember to recharge it.

I don't like people to be able to get at me. "Give me my scallop shell of quiet," as Sir Walter Raleigh (1552–1618) once said. By now, I've said it more than he ever did. Does that make it mine?

This aptitude for solitude is one of my most useful skills. It didn't happen all at once. Surely anyone who likes to read prefers to be alone and to sit still to do so. Those are preliminary requisites. It goes on from there, reaching the point of reclusiveness. I will have more to say about solitude in the course of my travels.

Now: sex. Here is where we separate the men from the boys and both from the women. Let me say it's a terrible thing for a woman to be widowed in her early forties.[5] The intense need/desire for sex in a woman that age is supposed to equal the hormonal rage of a seventeen-year-old boy. All those unbelievable stories you hear about older women and younger men are true, and if it happens to you, be grateful.

It's a difficult phase to live through without a companion. At first, one searches, mistaking lust for love, sometimes settling along the way for something short-term but tangible. Older men don't have that problem, never have. At whatever age, they don't seem to have any trouble finding willing, compatible younger women to satisfy their needs. They take it for granted. I remember my irritation with an older man (my age) who complained that he was getting tired of the "liver-spotted hand" laid so tenderly upon his. This meditation is not for him. Old geezers don't need any help, not for that, anyway.

Women are granted fewer appropriate outlets for their appeasement, whether sexual or companionate. At my age at that time, and in that decade, most men were a) married and either faithful or fooling around; b) divorced and either bitter or fooling around; or c) gay and either faithful or dying. Of the latter, several

---

[5] I was 42 when my husband suddenly dropped dead in front of me.

of the survivors became good friends of mine. Liaisons with the other two categories were not so successful.

Moving on.

I'm stuck in between "I can't go back" and "I can't go forward," not all the way. I have to stop short of the final frontier. I can't afford to waste time, because "at my back I always hear / Time's wingèd chariot hurrying near ..."[6]

In any case, the scallop shell is even quieter than it was before. I get fewer calls than I did because there are fewer callers. I am outliving my friends and family and furniture, as well as my doctors. Only the latter can be replaced, with difficulty, though, due to a shortage, and yet they are interchangeable and indistinguishable—or am I the only one who is unable to differentiate among these efficient scientists? They're all young. I do feel sorry for doctors today because our ailments are outpacing their knowledge. Never have so many people grown so old and lived long enough to develop maladies hitherto unknown to the medical profession.[7] All of us die, of course, some later than others, and we contribute to our doctors' knowledge of aging medicine.

So far, I seem to be later. I feel more and more like a duck in a shooting gallery, as my cohorts are being picked off around me.

Here is the best toast I have heard recently: raise your glasses to "absent friends." Of the absent, *nil nisi bonum*.[8] Good lines and voices remain in our heads and hearts, a capricious comfort, because they cannot be recalled at will and sometimes they come unbidden and not that welcome. Here's one, though, that has sustained me. It comes from the friend who said he would give me credit three times. When I was at a particularly low ebb of my life, he said to me: "You'll be all right, Betty Jane, because you have guts and grace."

---

[6] Andrew Marvell (1621–1678), "To His Coy Mistress."
[7] The song is older but the malady lingers on.
[8] "Of the dead, (speak) nothing but good."

Guts and grace.

The phrase became my rallying cry, not spurring me on but helping me to believe that I would survive. I suppose we all survive one way or another.

But not without love. I am still loved, though there is no one who would lose sleep or appetite over my passing. Just as well. I said when my husband died that I would not wish that pain on anyone. For my part, I love a number of people, though no one carnally.

We go on, we go on, and I intend to. We have met old people, to paraphrase from *Pogo*,[9] and they are us. I have a lot to say about them/us.

Age is another country, as it has been described for some 1500 years. And life, it has also been said for centuries, is a journey. Define "journey." From my online dictionary[10]: "trip, expedition, excursion, tour, trek, voyage, junket, cruise, ride, drive, jaunt, crossing, passage, flight, travels, wandering, globe-trotting, odyssey, pilgrimage, peregrination"—all of the above, but I draw the line at peregrination.

This is exciting, though. I'm not through yet. Does this make me a tourist? I don't think so. I prefer to call myself a traveller, and I am taking a long-term journey, through space and time, to the country of age. I'm there already. Gertrude Stein (1874–1946) said there is no "there there" but I'm here— or there— now. So I decided to write a book of essays, memories and responses pulled from my journey through life. This is not an autobiography. An autobiography is a life story, difficult and sometimes mendacious or fictionalized. Memoir is a collection of stories taken from the life journey, easier to write and forgivably embroidered. My memoir will comprise what I have picked up over the years, significant

---

[9]   *Pogo* was a comic strip by Walt Kelly (1913–1973). The line is "We have met the enemy and they are us."

[10]   *Oxford Dictionary of English,* current online version, 2015

moments in my life, but it is not a blow-by-blow account. It's a dipping book. Drop in anywhere, any time, and see what happens.

I may sound querulous from time to time, but I'm not angry. I actually began to write this book since before I was old, really old. Now that I am old, really old, the book I have written bears little resemblance to what I had in mind when I was sixty. Among other things, it has become, in part, a travel memoir; that is, travel into the past, which is a different country,[11] and also into that country of age, but not into the country after it,

"that undiscovered country from whose bourn no traveller returns".

William Shakespeare (1564–1616), *Hamlet*

---

[11] L.P. Hartley (1895–1972) begins his novel *The Go-Between*, published in 1953, with the line "The past is a foreign country: they do things differently there."

CHAPTER ONE

COUNTING

**If you live to be one hundred, you've got it made.
Very few people die past that age.**

George Burns (1896–1996)

Well, age is a numbers game. Right now we're on a winning streak, in good company and in goodly numbers. In fact, there are more people over 65 living today than in the entire recorded past. There have never been so many elderly people on this planet, and only about 5 percent of them are senile, despite what you have heard. Not only that, but contrary to what you may believe, the majority of them are living at home, not in institutions. The last American census was taken in 2010, the last Canadian one in 2011. Both countries are about to experience a tsunami of older people as the Boomers ride the wave. The first of the baby boomers turned 65 in 2011, with more to come. Their age group (which includes those born between 1946 and 1965) is increasing the fastest. The numbers are shifting. There are more Millennials, people who have come of age after the year 2000, than Boomers. One more surprising statistic when it comes to longevity: the lifespan of men is catching up to women's. The death rates among men have traditionally been higher, but as more men are living to older ages, the gap is closing. However, most elderly men are still married while most elderly women are more than three times as likely to be widowed and alone. The hard fact is that men have live-in caregivers, aka wives, and women do not. Still, older women generally prefer to live alone rather than in a home, as long as they can retain their health and independence.

These facts should be of interest to the young-old; that is, to the Boomers, people in their 50s and 60s, also known as The Sandwich Generation, layered as they are between the crusty, aging parents who didn't used to live so long and who now need attention and care, and the not-quite-baked children who are taking longer to get their education and to leave the nest (oven?) and be independent. So the middle age group is often spread painfully thin. For them, Freedom 55 is not so free and easy.

So far, I'm not telling you anything you don't already know. Life expectancy has been increasing one to two years per decade. It increases five hours a day! Isn't that ridiculous? It would seem that you have longer to live today than you did yesterday. What I find amusing is the promise made to people between 45 and 65 years of age that if they quit smoking or eat more wisely, they'll add 3 or 4 years to their lives. I already have. And if they exercise regularly, they'll reach their 80s (like me). So what are you going to do with all that extra time? Can you afford it? Do you have the energy and the cash to cope with it?

The real issue behind all the stats is actually money: income and investments and retirement plans and the high cost of aging. I've already written a book about retirement, so I won't go there. Just so you know, I'm aware of the problem that must be overcome or at least moderated on the dusty road to Nirvana. Readers of this book will have this basic problem more or less solved. They are concerned more about time than about money. How old do you want or expect to be? The usual legal age of retirement, changing gradually, is 65.[12]

There are three old age categories:

1) Young-old: 65–74 years
2) Old-old: 75–84 years
3) Oldest-old: 85 plus

Young-old age brings on the sunset years. Being a senior has definite perks as long as you're healthy and have your wits about you. That's the age I was when I first started thinking about this book. I enjoyed a fairly reliable amount of energy; a car, being frugal with the gas, not just for ecology's sake; a good appetite; my own teeth, give or take some root canals and crowns; senior discounts on movies and public transit; 20-percent-off days at local pharmacies; and some respect.

Respect, of course, isn't what it used to be when chivalry was in flower and gentlemen "protected" women—of a certain class. It was worse when women, according to the Canadian BNA Act (1867), for example, were ranked with imbeciles, lunatics and children, and had no privileges, only penalties. Of course, there are no guarantees of power or control, or even respect. I know that. Women do too. We'll see what happens as more of them are saying #MeToo.

A survey conducted by Larson Research Strategy in the United States December 2007 revealed that almost half of American women, ages 25 through 75, with an annual household income of at least $30,000, feared ending up as bag ladies. There was a line used during the Steinem years that most women were "one

---

[12] You may be familiar with the story of the Kaiser choosing the age at which his soldiers had to retire: 65, because few people lived past that and wouldn't have to be paid a pension for too long.

man away from welfare;" married women, that is. The Canadian magazine *Chatelaine* jumped on this in April of 2007 with an article by Carol Toller, who reported that Canadian women felt the same way; that is, they feared for their future and that they would end up living alone in poverty. Statistics still bear them out, though they're doing a little better than they did.

When I was doing the research for my book *Beginnings,* I found a statistic that has shifted slightly but is still valid: Of 100 women starting out at, say, age 20, 75 of them will be alone by the age of 65, whether widowed, divorced or never married. The divorced have traded places with the widowed in terms of numbers; the income of most of them has improved since I started keeping track, mainly because more women have worked outside the home and have some sort of pension plan or savings racked up. We go on, we go on, but not without difficulty. We're talking about survival here.

When I was doing research for my retirement book,[13] I met an affluent looking woman, late 40s, whose husband had just left her financially stranded. He had moved all his money to the Cayman Islands and left her in a big house in Rosedale with winter coming on and no cash to pay the heating bill. No one is secure.

The second stage of age, from 75 to 84, is old-old age. It was during this time that what I did in my formative and adult years became very important. In the days before pantyhose, my mother always made me wear over-pants, hateful things, and before that, long underwear—ugh— so I wouldn't ruin my kidneys. I should be grateful. My kidneys, I'm happy to say, function admirably. I keep remembering the comment by American composer Eubie Blake[14] on his hundredth birthday: "If I'd knowed I was going to live so long, I'd of taken better care of myself!"

---

[13]   *The Best is Yet To Come* (Key Porter Books, 1985)
[14]   James Hubert Blake, 1887–1983

Most women in the First World are like me: given a middle class background of comfortable means, we have enjoyed good nutrition all our lives, warm houses and warm clothes, and can count on several healthier, strong years. I just wish my mother had nagged me more about brushing my teeth.

I have noticed that age manifests itself in a slower recovery time. I have already noted that my well of energy is shallower than it used to be and when tapped, takes longer to refill. I thoroughly enjoy (need) an afternoon nap.

The oldest-old stage is what I call the "Twilight Zone," the era of life that gerontologists haven't solved yet, the years between 85 and forever. This is the after of forever after. I used to think that today was not forever, it only felt like it. Now I think today is quite fleeting, and forever is going to last quite a long time. I don't mind. I'm in no hurry. Not yet.

I think that apart from us old-timers, the ones who are most vitally interested in these statistics are the Baby Boomers, that generation we spawned. They are concerned with their parents' future, and for good reason. The bumper sticker, "We're spending our children's inheritance" on the back of a Florida-bound SUV, has an edge to it that becomes less amusing as the years go by.

"Reverse migration" is the term for a recent and increasing trend that sees elders return to their adult children, now their caregivers, they hope, as they outlive their energy and money. The truth is that most of the Freedom Fifty-Fivers never expected to live so long, nor did their children expect them to. Coming into the end zone is taking a lot of us by surprise. (I have to keep reminding myself how old I am.) Now our aging kids are looking at the future— both theirs and ours— with different eyes. The hard fact is that more people of both sexes are being given the

Chance to pass GO,[15] and the sad fact is that the going may be slow, shabby, sometimes painful and possibly boring, if we notice it. No one wants to play Beanbag Toss with a 90 year old. For that matter, 90 year olds are not too keen on Beanbag Toss, either.

Given that same good nutrition and vitality I have taken for granted all my life, I think that, barring accidents and the unforeseen, I'm going to "jangle along gently"[16] and slowly into that long goodnight. Given my druthers, I'd rather the final farewell be swift and dignified. "Dignified," said a character in the movie *All That Jazz* (1979), "means you don't drool."

Ah, but the mind goes on and on, even the one locked inside an Alzheimer's cellblock, subterranean and sweet, if not communicable. I visited Uncle Jim shortly before his death, imprisoned in a hospital bed and isolated by his deafness. He was a boy again, fishing in Scotland, with a river running through his mind.

We may all end up with fading memories and a short attention span. I'm going to worry about that later. The subject is me— you, us— now. I'm talking about my life and yours, about our long and lengthening life, and about living to a ripe, very ripe, old age. Good fruit doesn't fall off the tree, as the saying goes. I'm still in my tree, and I'm still playing the numbers game.

I've been a thinker and a communicator most of my life. Now I want to figure this out, figure out how age is, learn about it, the good, the bad and the ridiculous, the sweet, the bitter and the infuriating, and then I want to report back from the departure lounge before I take off on my final flight.

I promise I'll try not to complain, even as I point out inequities along the way. My comments are intended to be witty, caustic

---

[15] For my younger readers who have not spent their formative years playing Monopoly, I mean that we are taking the Chance card and keeping on keeping on.

[16] Attributed to the American baseball player, Satchell Paige (1906–1982)

but not self-pitying, and certainly not angry. I have nothing to complain about, and I know it. The last thing I want is pity. Forbearance is almost as bad. I have to be tough but ladylike because it's still a man's world (changing slowly?). Better to be witty than to seek pity. Just don't call me feisty.[17] And spare me from the birthday cake with NINETY YEARS YOUNG written on it in pink icing.

We all stand on the shoulders of giants, marking our progress from where we stepped on and staying longer. So there will be new discoveries and new connections and maybe some new conclusions; that is, if we live long enough. It's a numbers game.

Bear with me; the best is yet to be.
Robert Browning (1812–1889)

---

[17] From the German *fist*, meaning a small, aggressive and lively dog.

CHAPTER TWO

NEEDING

"How Much Land Does a Man Need?"
Six feet from his head to his heels was all he needed.

Leo Tolstoy (1828–1910)

In his book *A Good Age (1981),* Alex Comfort (1920–2000) says that there are four things a person needs to grow old comfortably:

- ✓ Dignity
- ✓ Money
- ✓ Proper medical care
- ✓ Useful work

Call the latter *occupation,* or *a goal.* I call it having a reason to get out of bed in the morning. After all, we're retired, most of us, so what's to stop us from lying abed in the morning? Comfort said the average length of retirement should be no more than two weeks, the length of a modest vacation. But he said that work need not be what we've been doing all our lives. He called a new occupation a "second trajectory"

He didn't mention companionship (of some sort or another, including dogs and cats), nice to have but not the most essential thing. I know some people who have never been alone in their entire lives. If/when they finally are really alone (bereaved), they have found it difficult, if not painful, to go solo. It is possible to fend for oneself; I'm living proof of that. It's another adventure, especially if it's well funded. And if it's not? More reason to get out of bed.

And what about travel? Again, there are different reasons for and attitudes to travel. Some people go just to say they've been. Been-there-done-that becomes a competition. When I hear someone say he's "done" a place, I wonder if the place has done anything to/for him. For some, it depends on one's age and income, one's health and energy, and one's imagination. Sometimes a trip to the drugstore can be a fascinating escapade.

I'm not very brave, and I don't like heights, but I am lured by what seems to me exotic, curious, romantic or unfamiliar. It doesn't have to be foreign or faraway or expensive. I love the Spadina streetcar because I get to ride on it down under the city street. I like bridges—not big, high, long or imposing ones—just little wooden ones over a stream in a park. I like stairs, not up the Eiffel Tower, but old stone steps worn into concave dents by centuries of feet—oh, and what about the double helix stairway in the Chambord castle in the Loire valley in France?[18]

Oh, the Places You'll Go![19]

More and more travel companies are offering single supplements, and some of them have even lowered the price somewhat. Some dream trips are best taken with a companion but some are perfectly possible as solo excursions. I have made good friends when I opted for a travel companion, but I have also enjoyed being single. It's another discovery. I'm glad, though, that

---

[18]   Designed by Leonardo da Vinci.
[19]   Title of the last book published in his lifetime by Dr. Seuss (1904-1991).

I went so late in life, after I had already developed self-confidence, a skill of solitude and also of eavesdropping—one of the real perks of being single, no matter where you go. People are always fascinating to listen to.

A long time ago now (1979), I went under cover for the *Toronto Star* to conduct some hands-on investigative research for a series of 5 articles that I called my "Old Lady Caper". I left home and went to live in a rooming house on the east side of Toronto. My sole income was OAS (Old Age Security); although the second week I found out about the Guaranteed Income Supplement and added that. My initial inspiration for the adventure came from a brochure entitled "Women and Poverty" (1979), written by a lawyer, Louise Dulude, for the recently formed National Council Status of Women Committee, funded originally by the Feds (under Brian Mulroney) but increasingly starved by later governments. It still exists now, surviving on membership fees and private donations. I can remember when I finished reading the piece I knew with absolute certainty what I had to do next: see for myself.

I found a place in a rooming house in the east end of the city, not far from Nellie's Women's Hostel, a short-term emergency centre. I had been warned to rent a place where there was a smoke detector in the hall and where the landlady lived in, preventing unwelcome visits from other lodgers. I shared a bathroom and a fridge in the hall with two men, each in a separate room, who stocked their side of the fridge with beer. I found a co-op store operating one afternoon a week in a nearby Senior Citizens' Centre where I could buy potatoes by the one, and I walked over to Nellie's every Sunday for big meat and conversation. I wanted the conversation more than the meat.

When I told my doctor what I was doing, he was concerned because at that time I tended to anemia. I described to him what I had been eating; he marveled, and said I couldn't have eaten better, that is, more nutritiously. I found out later that some high school students were assigned my published grocery list as a guide to shop and create meals.

My doctor gave me a list similar to Comfort's, of what he considered to be essential for older people:

- ✓ Money
- ✓ Security (same thing?)
- ✓ Health
- ✓ Companionship

It doesn't hurt to consider one's priorities: yours, mine, ours. We all have different needs and concerns. I guess my chief concern is for my challenged son, Matt, and my chief desire is for books. And good conversation. That means companionship. And interesting places to go and things to see. That means travel. It all requires money.

How much land does a man need? Less than you think. That was the point of Tolstoy's story. You don't need as much as you think you need, and it's dangerous to be blinded by greed. Financial planners used to tell clients, people who could afford financial planners, that they needed at least a million dollars in savings in order to retire with the lifestyle or comfort that they were currently enjoying, if, in fact, they were enjoying anything like that. Or, avoiding hard numbers, aim for 70 percent of former income to live in retirement. I read that they have revised that estimate downwards to 50 percent. That's closer. You won't need nearly as much as they think you'll need, mainly because your perceptions and needs will change.

My son Matthew has taught me that. He is challenged but "high-functioning".. He holds a part-time job at the top wage in his category, supplemented by a Disability Allowance that he dare not unbalance with overtime pay or he will be cut off until he has spent the money foolishly on food and rent. Yet he has a comfortable lifestyle and manages to save a little money for his old age, nothing like a million dollars, of course. He doesn't drink or smoke or party. He doesn't take pictures, and he doesn't read for pleasure, but he does watch movies and he has an enviable, even overwhelming, collection of DVDs and Blu-rays.

I watched my mother, who was left comfortable but not affluent, become very frugal out of apathy, not fear for her finances. She travelled for a while after my father died, but then she lost her nerve and her energy and she didn't want to go too far. She cancelled her last trip, a cruise, because she dreamed of her husband the night before, warning her not to go. The ship she was booked to go on ended up quarantined for some weeks with diphtheria on board. I'm just saying. What I am saying is that as she grew older and her finances dwindled, so, too, did her energy. She didn't feel like travelling any more, so she no longer needed money for travel.

You can cruise anywhere on the Net now. Armchair travellers can enjoy vicarious adventure and discovery in safety. I actually went to Africa to view wild animals coming to the salt lick at a Treetops location (my site was called The Ark), but you can watch them all day and night on your computer thanks to cameras set up in constant vigil. When my husband and I were young and poor, we used to travel in our kitchen. I would learn and cook the recipes indigenous to a country we were interested in. Even without leaving home, we found that travelling can be very broadening—that is, fattening.

After a certain age, though, money—that is, the need for it—can become a nagging problem and again; it affects women more than men. True, women are better off than when I was first widowed. At that time, a woman could earn about 63 cents of the dollar that men were paid. Did I say earn? No, that's all they were paid. They earned more than that. They still do, and after 40 years, they're up to about 73 to 78 cents on the dollar. Everyone thinks they have it made, including some women, the ones who have. More women are employed than men as I write this, but it's part-time work, generally, with no benefits and no pension plans, especially not portable ones. So where is the money for a leisurely retirement coming from? Let me count the ways:

- Try a reverse mortgage (if you own a house)
- Do some creative borrowing (buy a new sofa on time and use the cash to invest but check the interest rates; that is, if you really need a new sofa)
- Sell something (what's e-Bay for, anyway?)
- Downsize (more anon)
- Leave your credit card(s) at home one week a month
- Hesitate a day before you spend over 20 dollars (unless it's a limited-time bargain you can't ignore)
- Don't buy too much
- Pay off your debts (do I have to say that?)
- Use the float on your credit card (that's the gap between cut-off time and the next billing time)
- Take advantage of discounts
- Get rid of the car
- Barter
- Don't get sick

That's enough.[20]

I don't know how to make this any simpler. An analogy maybe. Beauty is in the eye of the beholder. Need is in the appetite of the hungry. It has to do with perception. It changes with age, if you're lucky. You're richer than you think.

God will provide –ah, if only He would till He does!

Yiddish Proverb

---

[20]   I wrote a book about enough: *Enough: Lifestyle and Financial Planning for Simpler Living*, Woodlake Books, 1999.

CHAPTER THREE

DOWNSIZING

**Anything you cannot relinquish when it has
outlived its usefulness possesses you
and in this materialistic age a great many of
us are possessed by our possessions.**

Peace Pilgrim (1908–1981)[21]

This chapter is about plethora and overage and pollution and ecology. I tried for 16 years to live a life of voluntary simplicity in a cottage by a lake. I came back to the city because the price of gas was escalating and I needed to be closer to my doctors and family.. In spite of having simplified my life, I still had a lot to move. I kept getting sidetracked and overwhelmed by possessions. Don't we all? What a mess!

The generic, public term is now "landfill." It used to be called a midden or a midden heap, often a shell midden, on coastal zones worldwide —piles of empty mollusk shells. I saw one once, on a beach on Galiano Island, a huge old mound of empty oyster

---

[21]   From 1953 to 1981, a silver-haired woman calling herself "Peace Pilgrim" walked more than 25,000 miles on a personal pilgrimage for peacepilgrim.org *Wikipedia.*

and clam shells in surprisingly good condition. There are also, according to *Wikipedia*, privy middens, self-explanatory, and packrat middens. Take note and take warning: "A packrat midden may preserve the materials incorporated into it for up to 50,000 years." That's the trouble with most detritus: it lasts for a long time.

We are in deep trouble. We all own too much and accumulate too much. We need help, we all do. Indeed, there are television shows devoted to helping hoarders stop hoarding, consumers stop consuming, and packrats stop packratting. People watch them, seeking salvation for their own sins of accretion and perhaps for pardon for their inability to let go.

Take hoard. Everyone does in one way or another. Hoarders were exemplary, like Aesop's ant that was much more prescient than the insouciant grasshopper, looking ahead to leaner times when the stash would be necessary for survival. People who were nervous about the millennium displayed admirable ant-like qualities, as they stored water and food and generators in case of power failures, but people who built fallout shelters during the Cuban Missile Crisis were considered callous toward their grasshopper neighbours.

And now? It's the ill-prepared neighbours of hoarders who are irritated at the mess next door.

What about consumers? The American economist Thorstein Veblen (1857–1929) coined the phrase "conspicuous consumption."[22] The term highlights the gap between the haves and the have nots that is wider today as the Occupiers glare at the one-percenters. On the other hand, we have contemporary social critic Paul Lukas, author of the book and coiner of the new

---

[22] Conspicuous consumption is the spending of money on and the acquiring of luxury goods and services to publicly display economic power—of the income or of the accumulated wealth of the buyer. *Wikipedia*.

phrase, *Inconspicuous Consumption: an Obsessive Look at the Stuff We Take for Granted, from the Everyday to the Obscure* (1997). His point? Nothing stays inconspicuous and nothing stays simple. But it stays.

A survey in the *New York Times* attempted a measurement of the storage space leased by people for their Stuff, but it was impossible to come up with exact figures since it grew faster than it could be measured. Hoarders, consumers, packrats and others cannot, cannot, cannot throw away what they own, even if they don't use it. No longer having any room left in their home for their Stuff, but unwilling to part with it, they rent storage space, huge lockers to store the overflow. They think they might use it some day, so they just keep on filling more space with more Stuff. Stuff happens.[23]

Stuff is what roots us to our family, not to mention basements, and now, storage lockers. Men don't leave home because they have their high school yearbooks; old unidentified pictures (and the negatives); significant champagne corks; historical front pages of newspapers; great centrefolds and a stamp album they abandoned when they were 11 years old. All this is packed in boxes that won't fit in a bachelor studio and would be too expensive for a rental locker should they ever move out, so they don't.

Women need storage not only for baby pictures and booties; report cards and kindergarten art work; old or odd earrings; obsolete keys and posh restaurant menus; and maybe the odd wedding dress, but also for the adult kids' Stuff they haven't moved out yet.

We all treasure mementoes from our past. We also hang on to things for the future just in case we'll need them, things like banquet-sized table cloths that don't fit any table we own; crystal ashtrays that are too good to toss even though no one smokes any more; four-tiered cake tins in the event one of the grandchildren

---

23   A euphemism if I ever heard one.

wants a home-baked wedding cake; a lopsided shelf that one of the kids made in shop class; a huge, classic covered roasting pan, though we don't eat much meat now and who could afford to buy a roast that big anyway?

You might be familiar with the Kitchen Test: putting kitchen gadgets in a box and hiding it for a year and if you don't need anything, toss it all. That's how I parted with my mushroom brush. But life is full of such tests and we are failing most of them. We are simply opting out, refusing to face worn-out, used artifacts. It's easier to hide them in closets or basements and to spend money on more storage space than to come to terms with our past. Well, everyone has a few precious items it would be unbearable to part with, unless forced. I read that the prairies during the time of the westward-moving wagon trains were littered with spinets and heirloom desks and family treasures that had become too heavy to carry. Hikers on the Chilkoot Pass, I am told, still carry too much Stuff and toss it into ravines to lighten their load. Most of us don't have that immediate, stressful need to divest ourselves of possessions/weight. If it took us half a lifetime to accumulate all the Stuff, it's going to take a while to unload it, and there is no single solution, Craigslist notwithstanding.

Getting rid of Stuff brings a complication no one has ever mentioned: searching for something after you've given it away. I think that might have more to do with one's short-term memory. It happens. Perhaps you, like me, find yourself looking for something you finally got rid of. That makes me think of a rule[24] I read: "The average length of time between throwing something away and needing it badly is two weeks. This time can be reduced to one week by retaining the thing for a long time first." Don't take this as a cue to buy a replacement. Stop and think why you tossed the thing in the first place.

---

[24]   One of *Bell's Rules,* from *The Official Explanations,* by Paul Dickson, Delacorte Press, New York, 1980.

There's a lot to say for recycling, and I haven't begun to contribute to the lore yet. I do recycle, and I profit by it as it makes me feel very moral and eco-friendly. There is an area in the underground garage in the apartment building I live in now designated for cast-offs, unwanted stuff too good for the garbage but that might appeal to someone else. It's called the Basement Boutique; some give it our street number to add a little cachet. It's amazing. I have given away some great stuff. I have also scored some great catches from it, items that leave me gleeful. It's a feeling that makes me understand the joy of dumpster diving. I've never done that, but I can see the appeal.

Everyone recycles now. I know of a famous recycling lifestyle that has gone on for years, on Hornby Island in British Columbia. Years ago, the enormous use the residents made of recycled material was honoured by an architectural magazine. "Home-Made Hornby" featured several houses built entirely of driftwood and, I guess, flotsam and jetsam, plus local contributions. There is a Free Store to which everyone donates, both goods and time. Volunteers sort and size and mend (in the case of clothing), clean and refurbish, if needed, and display the used wares for easy selection. I admired something in a local home and was proudly told that it was "bought" at the Free Store. While I was there, I also "bought" something and contributed a pair of jeans that needed a new zipper. (I can't sew.)

The economical re-use of goods has proliferated with the national consciousness of our need to be ecologically responsible. The Salvation Army and Goodwill have long been established as sources of re-used goods, oh, and Value Village. There are more outlets and sources now than ever before, on public and private levels. Everyone loves a bargain, especially if it's free. We would like to reduce our footprint on the planet and if we can do it comfortably and gainfully, all the better. Bolster your willpower. It takes courage and determination to get rid of Stuff.

We all get too much, own too much, use too little and accumulate constantly, and the older we grow, the more uncomfortable it becomes. For example, how many emery boards do you own, or nail clippers, stick pens, key chains, bottle openers, wine corks, calendars, notepads, razor blades, empty yogurt containers or pencil sharpeners? Of the latter, I found I had one blue, one red, one eyeliner sharpener, two swans and a duck. And I don't even use pencils. Most things are not our fault. They just have a way of piling up, through no failing of our own. It gets worse as we get older because people can't think of anything to give us because "we have everything."

World charities have suggested ways to avoid the unwanted accumulation of unnecessary stuff by asking for and giving in recipients' names donations—such as cows, goats, chickens, or contributions to wells and schoolrooms—to Third World people. This past Christmas, the first in the lives of my new great-grandchilden, I gave them blankets and mosquito netting.

Closer to home and the ubiquitous detritus,[25] it's possible to head off some stuff before it enters your home, like theatre programs (theatres now solicit the return of them as you exit), flyers and junk mail, and paper of all kinds. As a writer, I use a great deal of paper, but I try to use it all. I set my printer to print two sides for most documents. I write on the blank backs, and if they are partially used with some empty space remaining, I cut them into neat squares and keep my daily nags on them. It's such a pleasure to toss aside a chore accomplished. I used to have a fireplace; now I own a crosscut shredder whose mutilated contents go straight to the recycling bin.

It never stops, of course. The price of eternal vigilance is eternal vigilance. I just bought a whole box of paper and a box of 1000 business envelopes. Suddenly, I thought of green bananas. You are warned, as the cliché goes, that when you're as old as I am,

---

[25]   I know, it doesn't rhyme.

you should not buy green bananas because you may not be around long enough for them to ripen. So it is with paper. Will I still be around to use it all? As long as I keep writing I will.

Some people surround themselves with rubber bands; postal workers come to mind and Eloise, the fictional precocious little girl who lives in the Plaza Hotel and likes to twist a rubber band around her nose.[26] I do not consciously buy rubber bands, yet I seem to own more than I care to count. (How can anyone eat that much broccoli?)

We have to be vigilant, not only about conspicuous consumption but also about feverish frugality, which can lead to devastating detritus, which is not attractive. I knew a man who carefully folded and saved every brown paper liquor bag he ever acquired. He also had two drawers full of wine corks (I don't know what he does now with screw tops).[27] I also know someone who keeps his bread wrappers, crumbs and all. I have a friend who re-uses Post-it Notes, which is very conscientious, but what a clutter! Another woman I know saves all her empty yogurt cartons, and she eats a lot of yogurt. These are borderline nut cases, you say, you don't do that. Tell me: where does frugality stop and fetish begin? Look at the Collyer brothers.

For those too young to remember, the Collyer brothers, Homer (1881–1947) and Langley (1885–1947), were a pair of eccentric New York recluses who were discovered dead, trapped in the burrow of their Fifth Avenue home amidst a literal maze of newspapers and the accumulation of a lifetime. They had never thrown away a thing, including a Stutz Bearcat[28] in the living

---

26   Eloise was the subject of a series of children's books written in the 1950s by Kay Thompson (1909–1998) and illustrated by Hilary Knight (b. 1926). His portrait of Eloise hangs in the Plaza Hotel.

27   The reason I knew this was that I bought a credenza from him and he hadn't emptied his drawers.

28   A famous sports car, c. 1912.

room. This last detail about the car might not be true; I remember it from a novel, *My Brother's Keeper* (1954), by Marcia Davenport (1903–1996), based on the men's story, an urban legend in our time. I also saw a play about them by a playwright unknown to me who was trying it out in summer stock in Westport. More recently (2009), E. L. Doctorow wrote a bestseller titled *Homer and Langley* about the acquisitive oddballs. Imagine living like that! Yes, well, we all do, to some extent. Just look at the popular reality show *Hoarders*.

I have always held the Collyer example before me when too many things threaten to take over my world, and I know it is time to clear out my drawers.

"Remember the Collyer Brothers!" I shout and charge into battle with the bits and pieces of my life. (How about shards and orts?) I also take comfort from T. S. Eliot: "These fragments I have shored against my ruins." But I bet he didn't look at his drawers.

I've told this story before, but at my age I am entitled to a little repetition. I began my drawer-clearing habit when I was an undergraduate, performing a traditional act of attrition when I finished my exams each spring. Clearing out things was a metaphor for the clearing process going on in my brain.

Just before my last exam in my senior year, I made a bet with a friend I used to have coffee with that I would indeed clean out my drawers. To prove it when I did, I sent him seven discarded items, one from each of my desk drawers. I won my bet, and he took me to a movie. The only catch was, I married him a few years later and it turned out he was a packrat and still had those seven items, so they came back into my purlieu. I think that may be a cautionary tale, though it had a happy ending.

Years ago now—everything is years ago now, but this was 1997—when I divested myself of most of my large possessions in order to squeeze into a winterized cottage by a lake, I thought it was a one-time gesture. Cottages are not designed to store much; no provision is made for out-of-season clothes or luggage or Christmas decorations. Books are my biggest, most addictive accumulation, and they came with me, continuing to layer and multiply and spawn beyond reason. That means a lot of bookcases, and that means no wall or shelf space for paintings or ornaments. I gave stuff to charity flea markets and church bazaars and women's shelters. I sold my sterling silver flatware and Scottish crystal and bought a water pump with a hotline with the proceeds. I gave my china dinner sets to my daughters and my exotic utensils, like my oyster shucker and cornucopia bakers, to my adventurous son, but not my lemon zester or my grandmother's nutmeg grater. Some things are essential.

Simplification may begin with a massive clearing-out, but somehow it doesn't end there. As long as we go on living, we go on amassing stuff. The process goes on, and on, and on.

You know the old saying, "Three moves is as good as a fire." It suggests not only the inevitable loss and damage involved in a move but also the inexorability and the sense of powerlessness. Imagine how the victims of a flood or fire feel! When you downsize voluntarily along with your move, it's still havoc, and then you have only yourself to blame.

I'm not saying it's easy. At one point in my life I still owned every book I had bought, been given, or won as a prize. Facing my first major downsize, moving to Toronto after my husband died, I packed a few books destined for a Y book sale. In the middle of the night I woke up saying, "Elsie Dinsmore! I can't part with Elsie Dinsmore!" I did, though, and more besides. (And I regretted it.)

The point is that everyone has a few precious items it would be unbearable to part with. Don't part with them, then. Don't be too hard on yourself. Be realistic about your needs and also your wants. You're not going to be happy if you feel deprived. After all, it took you half a lifetime or more to accumulate all this stuff; you're not going to get rid of it overnight. Nor should you allow yourself to feel like a victim. No matter what the reasons for this process of elimination, you'll be happier to look on it as an adventure, a wonderful opportunity to begin again, a chance to ignore your past mistakes and to make new ones.

Perhaps it was easier for me to eliminate the negatives because I was alone. Couples have to respect each other's foibles and addictions, make allowances and room for them. Couples also have to give each other space, not just for their things. I have a friend who lives in a 3-storey, 10-room house and jokes that when her husband reaches full retirement, they'll have to move to a bigger house. Only I don't think she's joking. The old line about "for better or for worse, but not for lunch" often holds true. People need a place where they can be free from each other. You should keep that in mind if you're hunting for a smaller home. With some forethought it may be possible to make a quiet retreat for one or the other to use separately when the need to escape is urgent. It takes a little ingenuity, and you might have to lose weight.

I know one man who fitted an entire office into a closet. He took off the door, removed the clothes rod and overhead shelf, measured carefully and installed what he needed without resorting to custom-built carpentry. I know a single woman who stores her tools—hammer, wrench, screwdriver and such—in a pretty basket on her living room floor. It's right under a slightly smaller basket holding her notepaper, chequebook, envelopes, stamps, bills and ballpoints. You can tell she's older and doesn't own a computer.

There are entire shops now devoted to closets and storage solutions and inexpensive furniture designed for small spaces (some assembly required), as well as for large storage needs. Does anyone remember the Murphy bed? I, of course, am too young ever to have owned one, but I saw them in old movies. It's a bed that pulls down out of the wall. They're still being made, and they are much more handsome and useful now. A retired couple I know, who moved into a much smaller space, bought a modern bed-in-a-wall for their spare room. Hidden away, the bed is a part of a wall-width storage unit with an attractive door on which is anchored a painting (so it doesn't fall off when the bed comes down), flanked by bookcases and a drop-leaf desk. When the bed is not in use, the entire room is a functional office.

Not all apartments have a balcony. I have one and I call it my summer cottage. With a little care, it becomes an outdoor living room in the summer, and it's a great place to work and eat and garden. I have a friend who gardens on her balcony and gets more ambitious every year. She makes her own mulch. Last year, she grew tomatoes and installed a little wall fountain. She may start a small vineyard soon.

One of the hazards of moving has always been the difficulty in finding things in the new place. I can still remember where I put stuff in my very first house, though I sometimes have difficulty putting my hands on something I bought last week. I know this has more to do with my short-term memory rather than the long-term effects of moving. Getting rid of stuff when you move adds another complication: you find yourself looking for something you gave away. Don't take this as a cue to buy a replacement. Remember Bell's Rule.

Speaking of tossing, one of the joyous post-pitch experiences is the realization that *you don't have to keep things*. After my major purge, which included a lot of mementos from a lifetime of saving paper and souvenirs,[29] I went on a trip. I was on the other side of the world, literally (New Zealand), and I had an accumulation of things on the hotel dresser when I was packing to go home. I picked up a menu, a brochure and a theatre ticket and tossed them in the waste paper basket. *At last*, I thought, *I'm free*! I have a friend who scoffed at me. "Stop picking them up in the first place," she said. Ah, but I take information from them for my travel journal for my report, to check spelling for my nitpicking.

---

[29] The other great way of clearing with a clear conscience is to donate things to archives. The University of Manitoba has been good enough to take my leavings.
You can look it up—they're called "fonds."

Such an enlightening way to travel can begin before you leave, too. I met a young couple when I went to South America who had bought good used clothes in thrift shops, wore them and left them in their hotel room as usable tips for the staff. I thought that was a brilliant idea and when I went to Russia, I did the same thing but I used my own clothes: a pair of Rockport shoes with lots of wear left in them, a Ralph Lauren denim skirt that was too long for me, a Shetland cardigan with one button missing (I don't sew, so I also left a travel sewing kit). Downsizing is a wonderful way to acknowledge, and also take advantage of, one's increasing foibles and advancing years.

One thing no one mentions is the fear factor. People groan in sympathy at the thought of all the work that goes into downsizing, but most of them, unless they've lived through it, are not aware of how terrifying it is. Like me and Elsie Dinsmore. Do you really want to go through the rest of your life without steak knives?

I seldom used my steak knives, with their lovely Sheffield steel blades and stag handles, because I was afraid of putting them in the dishwasher. Just recently I decided that they would last longer than I would, and I began to use them regularly, even when I didn't have steak, so I put them in the machine. They're fine. So am I.

Midas's Law:
Possession diminishes perception of value, immediately.

John Updike (1932–2009), *Problems and Other Stories*

CHAPTER FOUR

HITTING THE ROAD

Travelling is a fool's paradise … I pack my trunk, embrace my friends, embark on the sea and at last wake up in Naples, and there beside me is the stern fact, the sad self, unrelenting, identical, that I fled from.

Ralph Waldo Emerson (1803–1882)

It depends on how much you like yourself whether, no matter where you go or how far, you are pleased or dismayed to discover that you can't escape. You take you with you, even if you're not sure who that is. Some people don't want to know and do their best always to be busy, never to be alone. It's amazing how well they manage to do this. I, on the other hand, struggle to clock enough solitary hours with myself. I love to travel, though. The inveterate traveller, Paul Theroux says, "if you're afraid of loneliness, don't travel." Maybe that's why I love it.

I'll deal with solitude later. Right now, I want to consider how travel affects us. Have you ever been told you look rejuvenated after a trip? Maybe not. Travel can be an ordeal that affects us, ages us, in fact. It's stress, albeit stress of your choosing, usually, and with whatever level of comfort you can afford. The best-laid plans go oft awry, and you can end up stranded and far from silent upon a peak in Darien, demanding that someone do something feeling the wrinkles popping out on your face. Travel is not easy, not these days, and the single supplement doesn't help.

A few intrepid ladies in the 19th century travelled alone, like Isabella Bird (1831--1904), for example, alone on a horse in the Rockies and loving every vista, according to her enthusiastic diary; or Freya Stark (1893–1993), who reveled in exotic travel,[30] to put it mildly. She summed up her attitude in a few words: "To awaken quite alone in a strange town is one of the pleasantest sensations in the world."[31] I like it too, though I often have to get my bearings and remember where I am. Compared to others' adventures, what I have done is bland toe-dipping in a wading pool, casual stops on the way to the ultimate trip.

Many travellers agree that the inner journey is the most revealing and hazardous one. However, a French military man introduced "a new mode of travelling into the world," just for fun. Xavier de Maistre (1763–1852) is known best as the creator of a strange travel book he wrote when he was placed under house arrest for dueling. *Voyage autour de ma chambre* describes the objects in his room as if he were encountering them in a voyage to a strange country. It's a cheap trip, good for poor or lazy travellers.

"When I travel through my room, I rarely follow a straight line: I go from the table towards a picture hanging in a corner; from there, I set out obliquely towards the door; but even though, when I begin, it really is my intention to go there, if I happen to meet my armchair en route, I don't think twice about it, and settle down in it without further ado."[32]

---

[30] And wrote more than two dozen books on her travels in the Middle East and Afghanistan.

[31] From https://www.burgerabroad.com/stark-quotes/

[32] Quoting from *Wikipedia*.

De Maistre wrote this to keep boredom at bay, but his brother Joseph liked it and convinced him to publish it in 1794. The really strange thing about this send-up of a trip is that it matches a pattern followed by political prisoners today in their attempts to keep fit and sane during much longer periods of confinement. A trip around a room can become a journey round the world, with survival as its goal.

People travel for different reasons. The addicted ones, like me, say they do it— "doing it" meaning, in part, putting up with awkward airplane arrangements, lost luggage, bumpy buses, skewed schedules and strange travelling companions— for the sake of a new experience, either visual or (best of all) emotional, something that they have never encountered before. If they keep on doing it, they discover something else, the real reason that keeps them searching. That reason has to do with what's going on in the landscape of their minds. This is what I call "personal geography," my own private map, very much part of my travel memoir and useful not only for the memories gathered but also for the insights garnered.

Historical maps drafted by ancient cartographers are fanciful and sometimes lurid, complete with fat-cheeked faces blowing wind in several directions and with wavy lines above a queasy sea spelling out dire warnings: "Here be sea serpents." My personal map keeps changing with my continuing, if limited, exploration of the planet. I've seen zebras in Africa and icebergs off Greenland and winds around the Jungfrau. I've cheered on a very young albatross attempting its first takeoff from a fresh tarmac in southern New Zealand; been turned on by the long, slow, relaxed coitus of two tortoises on a lagoon in one of the Galapagos Islands; watched the sun rise over Machu Picchu from the place photographers stand to take the famous picture that lured me there in the first place. (I don't take pictures but I wanted to stand there.) I also stood under a waterfall (Seljalandsfoss) in Iceland, feeling like a troll and getting mildewed; and in spite of my fear of heights, I climbed down a rough wooden ladder thousands of feet above the Earth's floor to inspect the penthouse dwellings of the Anasazi at Mesa Verde.

When I saw the mysteriously abandoned homes of the Anasazi, another one of those astonishing signposts fell into my head to teach me something I didn't know I knew. It read:

PEACE

3 kilometers
OR
10 centuries

WHICHEVER COMES FIRST

The world is so much with us today, so seemingly familiar, that we forget how foreign it is. We meet a past that has disappeared but that nevertheless forces us into a space-time continuum where eternal moments stand still and only people move.

"Been there, done that." It's one of the more annoying comments a jaded know-it-all tourist says about trips she's already taken. The difference between a tourist and a traveller, the professional traveller, Paul Theroux points out, is that "tourists don't know where they've been; travellers don't know where they're going." Too glib? Perhaps. But the late composer and writer Paul Bowles (1910–1999) agreed with the distinction: "He did not think of himself as a tourist; he was a traveller." We may not know which we are until we get there, wherever there is.

In the meantime, we keep searching, because whether tourist (voyeur) or traveller (observer), the journey is always a quest, the ultimate search for self.

And so it was for me, clambering around that Anasazi cliff dwelling. It was like creeping into a time machine and falling back—or up— into an alien past. High on a ledge in the middle of nowhere, having slipped down through clefts and narrow stone walkways and scrambled up a series of switchbacks to the cliff-side condo, I was then expected to lower myself through a trapdoor and feel my way down a wooden ladder into a dark kiva—a place of worship cut deep into the rock. Then— as if I had a choice—I wiggled through a tight-fitting tunnel, cut for people with narrower hips than mine, emerging in an annex, thence to shinny up a short ladder to a room with a view. Given a physical site like that, anyone can project into the past. The real wonder is how you get back, both mentally and physically. In my case, my fear of heights, as I mentioned, warred with my lust for experience. Lust won. There I was, slip-sliding down a crevice and then cling-climbing up a 3-storey wooden ladder set halfway up the cliff, taking us away from the airy dwelling we had just visited.

The next assault was directed at the top of the mountain. After the ladder, I teetered up a rocky staircase, if the rough surfaces could be called stairs, hedged by a frayed chicken wire railing that quivered between me and the valley floor two thousand feet below. I left my fear behind and took with me the memory of a clear pool at the back wall of this mountain home, the water in it supplied by seepage through the rock from rain on the plateau above. With running water, no flies, no pests, human or animal, natural air-conditioning and lighting supplied by the Designer, the ancient apartment building revealed an 11th-century plan for living. In North America, that is. Everything is relative and affects our understanding. Consider:

At roughly the same time in Europe, Ethelred II was paying the Danes protection money, but the Danes took over England anyway. Henry I became King of France in 1030 and Malcolm II of Scotland was succeeded by his grandson Duncan, the one who was later murdered by Macbeth.

How much we have changed! How much have we changed?

The Anasazi knew nothing of all that. As suddenly as they appeared, they seem to have vanished from the mountaintops, and no one knows why. They were the first high-rise apartment dwellers, with one eye for beauty and one for safety—safety from animals and enemies, that is. As for heights, they must have had no fear and no vertigo, none at all, and neither do their down-to-earth descendants. My discovery of them and their place in the timeline of world history leaves me with some inkling of the negligible place where I fit in—and very humble.

An experience of time warp was handed to me the day we drove up a mesa to a Hopi village, one of the oldest still inhabited. From a noisy 20th-century street festival in a remote spot supplied with electricity and Coca Cola, we took a 10-minute walk into the past: no power, no running water, but two active kivas where the men still gathered to worship and where women were allowed for only a very few special occasions during the year. This time travel in microcosm provided greater insight into the ancient ones' cliff palaces we had just finished exploring. Not to over-simplify, because the world and its people have changed radically since the 11th century, but the existence of those ghost-inhabited cliff houses gave me a glimpse of the past and some of my hitherto unknown ancestors and a kind of fragile continuity: space-time, as I finally understood it.

This is a view familiar to the Incas and the peoples of the Andes, and so, perhaps, to the Anasazi? To me, it's a clue to my life-journey. My consciousness moves along a linear lifeline, but because I've lived so long, events seem to be closer together, even simultaneous, or maybe they move along a Möbius Strip, one of my favourite concepts: it's a ring with only one side. If you move along it far enough, you'll return to your starting point without ever leaving that side or surface. It's a simple illustration of a time machine. The idea suits my travel memoirs; all time is present. It helps if your memory is still functioning.

Psychiatrist Viktor Frankl (1905–1997) didn't write travel books, but his accounts of his Holocaust experience provide another clue to the assimilation and reconciliation of time with the events of our lives that we all must attempt in our long journey. He noted that, generally, those who had a reason to keep on living did so because their purpose gave them a goal beyond mere survival. He developed a theory to support this idea: "Live as if you were living already for the second time and as if you had acted the first time as wrongly as you are about to act now!"

It's double vision, better than binoculars for the kind of sightseeing I'm doing, a kind of hindsight with foresight attached, or maybe—better— I need a new stereopticon to see life in all its dimensions. I think I am going to achieve a view of my life journey. I just have to hang in there, preferably with memory intact.

There is no there there

Gertrude Stein (1974–1946)

CHAPTER FIVE

AGING

**When people tell you how young you look,
they are telling you how old you are.**

Cary Grant (1904–1986)

When you're as old as I am, most strangers tend to talk to you the way they do to little kids—more like in front of or about, rather than to you.

"My, isn't he big for his age?"

"She's really quite bright for her age."

"They'll be in school before you know it."

There isn't quite the same optimism or approval in the words addressed to (aimed at) us older kids. Some doubt lingers:

"You look pretty good for your age."

"Eighty-eight? You'd never know it."

"Can you still drive? Can you hear okay?"

It's called "Elderspeak," and it is unbearable. Everyone, it seems, is hardwired into stereotypes. It's becoming difficult, being treated like that, not to fall into them. We've all been living too long in Disneyland or Rockwell country, where old people are one-dimensional clichés. Remember Norman Rockwell?

It's too easy to generalize about Norman Rockwell (1894–1978), but his influence was powerful. He portrayed old people, among others, both male and female, as lovable examples of perfect grandparents. He and his subjects were typecast. For years he was dismissed as a mere illustrator (as he called himself), not an artist. He sentimentalized and idealized his subject: American Home Life. In 1977, he actually received the Presidential Medal of Freedom, the highest civilian honour in the U.S., for "vivid and affectionate portraits of our country," ones we all recognize, even if we're Canadian.

Hollywood helped perpetuate the myth, too, with icons of adorable old folks. I'm so old I can remember some of their names: Lionel Barrymore (Andy Hardy's father); Edmund Gwenn (everybody's favourite Kris Kringle, aka Santa Claus); Donald Crisp (in *How Green Was My Valley* and *Lassie Come Home*).

The more contemporary portrayals of older people tend to be less limiting. No longer are characters confined to the role of endearing grandparent. Ian McKellen's Gandalf and Michael Gambon's Albus Dumbledore, for example, largely avoid the stereotypes forced upon their predecessors. The women used to be noted for their sympathetic behaviour, not crusty like the men but occasionally ditzy: Spring Byington (*You Can't Take It With You*); Billie Burke (Clara Topper, Glinda, the Good Witch of the North); and Faye Bainter (Mrs. Gibbs in *Our Town*). There's Maggie Smith, of course, an outspoken dowager in *Downton Abbey,* and tough-minded witch Minerva McGonagall in the Harry Potter series; Judi Dench, flinty as M in the Bond films and lovable but practical as Evelyn Greenslade in *The Best Exotic Marigold Hotel.*

I also note that most of the names I mentioned (and had to look up) are well-trained actors, frequently British. They grow older, but they don't get typecast. That's good for them, but it hasn't penetrated the minds of their audiences or our caregivers—and especially not those of the moviemakers, at least not yet. I still maintain that mothballs and clichés still cling to older people on whatever path of life they walk. It's easier to make a snap decision based on habit than to assess people we meet on their own terms. But, oh, how tired I am of being called "dear" by women and "young lady" by men! I am neither, and similarly fed up is an older man addressed as "sir," no respect intended. "Senior citizen" isn't much better. They don't mean senior; they just mean old, as in aged.

What about Disney? Apart from the damaging myths that "someday my Prince will come" and "be good and you'll be taken care of," he perpetuated some terrible propaganda about witches. They've had bad press from day one,[33] and they're still getting it. Now that Greek or Norse or Judeo-Christian mythology gets so little recognition, fairy tales supply a common base for modern grim stories. There are *Once Upon a Time* and *Grimm*, both fairly recent TV series roughly based on fairy tales, and any number of Hollywood movies based on Snow White (*and the Huntsman; Mirror, Mirror*), Hansel and Gretel (*Witch Hunters*), and more to come, I'm sure; plus there's a whole sub-category of Cinderella lore, not quite as gruesome as the others, although the stepmother is nasty. In all the accounts, old women, stepmothers, witches and hags are interchangeable and get instant condemnation and no sympathy at all. They are mean, vicious, cruel and ugly, even glamorous ones like Charlize Theron. They are all OLD, even Theron. Behind that lovely, unnaturally young face lurks a centuries-old creature. One of the most ubiquitous images of a witch that comes to everyone's mind is that of Margaret Hamilton (1902–1995), who played the Wicked Witch of the West. Her terrifying cackle became part of children's nightmares. She was just 36 when she appeared in the film *The Wizard of Oz* (1939), considered a classic now and aired regularly on TV. Hamilton's witch was aged, now ageless. Too bad.

---

[33] *The Malleus Maleficarum* (1496) is the best-known of the witch-hunt manuals.

Of course the images affected me, all of us. Still do. I was guilty of easy denial for quite a while. I inherited good skin and a youthful appearance from my Icelandic ancestors. It helped that I was accelerated in school, starting university at the age of 15. So I was always 2 years younger than my peers. I never lied about my age, as my mother's generation did. I just detached myself from the clichés and never talked about it. I had a close friend, a model whose face was her fortune, who lectured me not to remember too well.

✓ "You must learn to say, with irreproachable innocence, "Who's Warner Baxter?"[34]

"You can never be too rich or too thin," said the Duchess of Windsor (1896–1986). Or too young?

It's not all Disney's fault. Stats Canada supplies the definition of sociogenic aging. It reads like folkloric stereotypes to me.

THE DEFINITION:

Sociogenic aging: ageism that is imposed upon the elderly by the beliefs and values, folklore, myths, prejudice, stereotypes, etc. that prevail in society, e.g. slow drivers, not very good with technology, forgetful, religious.

Bio-medicalization of aging: the belief that problems associated with aging are biological rather than social or behavioral.

How can I win?

Well, I look pretty good, but no one tells me that. People, particularly women, don't tell other women that they look beautiful or pretty or even nice until they're too old to be considered competition (for what?). They say, if they feel compelled to say

---

[34] Warner Baxter (1889–1951), an American film actor from the 1910s to the 1940s. He was the second actor to win an Oscar at the second Academy Awards for the movie *Old Arizona* (1928).

anything, "you look healthy, or fit," meaning, quite often, fat. Or they say, "you look young," thereby telling you, as Cary Grant has pointed out, that you are old. Or they say, if you really are old, "you don't look a day over 70." Hell! You wanted to look 35. Until you don't—want to, that is. There came a day, sometime in my early eighties, I think, when I reconciled myself, quite happily, I might add, to being old, even to the point, as I have said, that I brag about it. I have known some women who have even added a few years. It's a matter of, according to a birthday card, not how old you look but how old you feel, and that's purely arbitrary. If you're healthy, you feel pretty young, comparatively speaking, and look it, too. Looking young has to do with vitality and projection.

A few years ago, I ripped the meniscus in my right knee. "Meniscus" was a new word to me. I had never been much of an athlete, but now I'm taking exercise seriously, and my body does too, hence the knee problem. That's when I got to say one of my favourite lines. The examining doctor asked me how old I was. I was 72 at the time. He shrugged, murmuring something to the effect that you have to expect a knee problem at my age. And I said, "My left knee is also 72, and it doesn't hurt." See? It's part of the stereotype: you get old, you get sore. (Suck it up.)

The meniscus eventually stopped bothering me because I didn't take painkillers. I exercised instead. No one tells old people to do that; doctors don't. They give everyone a prescription and dismiss the case. Next. I did use a cane, as briefly as possible. I went to my own doctor to report the results from the emergency clinic I had raced to, in a manner of speaking, and he actually told me I looked frail. Frail!! A big, strapping girl like me? It was the cane, of course—another stereotype. Lean on a cane, look frail.

When my mother died, I looked at her lying on the hospital bed as I waited for her to be processed. Suddenly she appeared smaller, much more fragile than she had seemed. I realized then that her spirit had projected more energy than she possessed and had made her appear larger than—life? Larger than death, I guess. Aesop was right: appearances can be deceiving.

But so can expectations, and they can have a negative effect. If you expect to fail, you probably will. If you expect someone else to fail, she won't disappoint you. It pays to keep your hopes up. Even if you fall short of expectations, your score will be higher than if you started out expecting zero.

Expectations can be as damaging as stereotypes. There's a double standard at work here, too; they're more detrimental to women than to men.

Anyone who works a few crossword puzzles knows that "crone" is a synonym for old woman, hag or witch, sometimes virago, although that word was at one time complimentary, stemming from the Latin for man (*vir*) and describing a strong female warrior. Usually, though, virago means a domineering, violent, or bad-tempered woman. Even gossip, the dear old soul, is now dismissed as a gabby old woman who jabbers about other people's private lives. "Gossip" originally derived from the late Old English "godsibb," from "god," God, plus "sib," which meant a relative, someone related to God, a godmother or godfather, a baptismal sponsor, and a very respectable person. What a demotion for the old biddy (there's another one). And the verb, "to gossip," has nothing respectable about it, with connotations of untruth, exaggeration and salacious material.

Mary Daly (1928–2010), the feminist academic and theologian, managed to infuse new meaning into many of the derogatory words referring to women. She said, "A woman becomes a Crone as a result of Surviving early stages of the Otherworld Journey and therefore having discovered depths of courage, strength, and wisdom in her Self." (Caps hers.) Hags are holy and viragos are warriors, as I said, and not shrews. Stereotypes can be damaging. So, crone, hag, witch—no longer the Angel of the House but unfortunately still the Angel of Death, the Queen of Spades, Queen of Witches, Hecate. (Remember Hecate, standing at the crossroads, watching all the men go by?) All the labels and epithets can be self-fulfilling and should be recast and rethought. I can't be the only one who thinks that the image of the older woman needs improving—no—refurbishing. At least "crone," thanks to Daly, has been nobly recovered (outside of crosswords) and has become a respectful name for a strong, proud, older woman. It's about time to restore meaning as well as dignity to our declining years.[35] I'm doing my best. You can help.

The poet Samuel Taylor Coleridge (1772–1834) said there are three kinds of elderly woman: "that dear old soul; that old woman, and that old witch." I don't think "dear old soul" serves her much better than "witch." In this century, as in others, dear old souls get mugged and beaten and robbed, not revered, while old witches are shunned and shoved aside, though not burned. Whatever happened to the "wise blood" of the old woman once she started saving it up after menopause? It seems to have dried up and left the image of a shriveled old woman behind.

In my play *A Place on Earth* (1982),[36] Peggy Woodgreen, an old woman living in a room, has received plastic fangs in the mail, a Halloween present from her granddaughter. When some neighbourhood boys start catcalling outside her window, "Wood green is a wi-itch. Woodgreen is a wi-itch," she remembers her fangs, inserts them and opens the curtain to screech and snarl at the boys, who run away. Laughing and triumphant, she turns away from the window and pauses a moment before she says thoughtfully, "In another century I'd have been burned as a witch." It's the image we still can't shed.

Knights and witches; the double standard continues, particularly when applied to aging. Silver-haired men are distinguished; grey-haired women, whether blue-rinsed or apricot-highlighted, are simply faded. But older men are now getting their

---

35 There's a magazine called *Crone: Women Coming of Age*, launched in 2008.
36 First produced in 1982, published by Playwrights Press in 1995.

share of disparaging terms. DOM (Dirty Old Man) is the most common, but consider "coot" (usually an old one), fossil, geezer, codger and curmudgeon—this latter term is occasionally unisex but more often assigned to men. Sometimes an aging, timid man is called an "old woman." Not kind to either gender. The adjective "feisty," on the other hand, is more commonly applied to women. Interestingly, in the late 19th century, "feist" was a small dog, and it was a derogatory term for a lapdog, from the Middle English "fist," meaning to break wind. I suppose that's where "old fart" comes from (more frequently referring to a man).

There is a point to all this etymology. I am dealing with ageism; that is, prejudice or discrimination on the basis of a person's age. It can be very costly for a man. Workplace claims on the basis of age discrimination have increased over the past several years, but redress is hard to achieve, harder, apparently, than for black-versus-white or male-versus-female claims of bias. The official age for retirement is changing, not simply because the aging employee doesn't feel that old but also because he wants to keep working and earning money. Younger workers, on the other hand, wish he would quit so they could earn his higher salary. On the other other hand, employers like the thought of paying a less-experienced worker less money. The numbers involved exacerbates the general situation. Once again, the Boomers are skewing the statistics. They are the new greying generation; they are healthier and likely to live longer, so they want to be working longer. The younger ones coming on resent this, hence the discrimination.

It has become a commonplace, almost accepted fact, that a man in his mid-fifties who loses his job may never work again, or may take twice as long as a younger man to find a new job and almost certainly will never recover his former earning power. Bias can be damaging, not only financially but also psychologically.

That old question to a retired person, especially to an aging boomer, can really hurt: "Who did you used to be?"

As for the women, the emotional and psychological injury is not visible. Sadly, neither is she. It's a shock to discover that one is invisible.

At first, I wasn't aware of what had been happening. The changes had been very gradual. I thought perhaps construction workers had become more polite. On the whole, one doesn't miss catcalls. As for the gropers on the subway, it had become second nature to use effective deterrents like a big coat or an armload of books or groceries or a well-placed (high) heel. For that matter, I couldn't remember when I had last heard a sailor whistle, but then, there hadn't been a war for a long time. Then, it dawned on me: it was I, not they. I was the one who had changed. Men hadn't forgotten how to whistle, nor were they feeling especially threatened by sexual harassment suits. (They used to get off. No more.)

But that was not the case; I had simply become invisible. Actually, sound leaves before sight.

"That's the third time you've interrupted me this evening," I said to a man at a party a couple of years before that revelation.

"What did you say?" he asked. "I didn't hear you."

He didn't, either; he really didn't. Men don't. They don't hear or see women most of the time, unless they want something. Females of a certain age are both inaudible and invisible to most males. Regrettably, there's no way to sue for sexual non-harassment.

It's not that I miss the gauntlet of men's eyes. I can still remember how careful I had to be, how prim and rigid, looking neither left nor right, pretending I was deaf, being such a lady that I couldn't possibly understand the comments and innuendoes. As much as I like the composer Frank Loesser (1910–1969), I hate his song with the lyrics, "Standing on the corner/Watching all the girls go by" (from *Most Happy Fella,* 1956) with its arrogant assumption that girl watching and catcalling and date-baiting were a man's pleasure and privilege.[37]

---

[37]   Oddly enough, the pleasure is mine now, and the privilege: to be anonymous and unnoticed, to be less threatened because I am invisible.

I have heard and read other women's complaints, women who resented this erasure as yet another example of the double standard of aging. It seems that men don't grow old, they grow distinguished,[38] if they're rich enough, but almost all women don't grow old, they disappear. Out of sight, out of mind. Certainly, in terms of the dating and mating market, age is a handicap to a mature woman when all the mature (rich) men are getting it on with the nymphets and trophy wives, and the women their age are cast in the role of a Dear Abby.

I myself sat through several lunches with at least three different men my own age, listening as they confessed their delight in their newfound love. With insensitive glee, they reported their rejuvenation and resurrected virility, raised, so to speak, from the dead by a young woman their/my daughter's age. At least they bought lunch.

I do think that every mature woman is entitled to at least one shot of her own at the nursery, and I'm not talking about babies. It's an ego trip, to be sure, to date a younger man, but it can be humiliating to have to teach a Significant Kid the words to the Muzak on the elevator or in the supermarket.

I must admit that younger men can be very sweet, not quite as spoiled (by us) as the older ones. And they—the ones who like older women—like to listen to us, at least part of the time. They don't mind our knowledge or our wisdom. Nice while it lasts. But nothing lasts. It is with something like relief that one drifts back into invisibility; relief because it can be very tiring. As a contemporary said to me, after she had ruefully but gracefully let her toyboy slip-slide away, "At least now I don't have to hold my stomach in all the time. It was such a strain."

Oh yes, a strain! The nip-slash-tucks,[39] the hair tinting, the makeup, most of which turn a perfectly respectable old woman

---

38 Their hold is loosening, I'm happy to say.
39 Did you know that a genuine face-lift works on the same principle as prepping a Peking duck? The skin has to be lifted away from the flesh; butchers have to be careful not to puncture the skin.

into a drag queen, not because she wants it but because in some circles it seems to be expected of her. Hard lines!

When my model friend subjected herself to a face-lift, I quoted *The Book of Samuel* to her (Chapter 16, vii):

> But the Lord said unto Samuel, Look not on his countenance, or on the height of his stature; because I have refused him: for the Lord seeth not as man seeth; for man looketh on the outward appearance, but the Lord looketh on the heart.

I look my age now, and it's okay. I ignore the lotions, creams and emollients (nice word) on offer for a price that promises to soften—not erase—the *appearance* of wrinkles. Let the wrinkles fall where they may. Surely they indicate I have lived my life and have something to show for it. Wisdom?

In T. S. Eliot's play *The Family Reunion* (1939), Harry, the oldest son of a matriarch, returns after 8 years away to a family reunion celebrating her birthday. My copy of the play, purchased when it was published, cost 2 dollars, no tax— old, like me. After all these years, I thought I remembered a line Harry says to his family:

"You all look so wrinkled and so young."

But the word wasn't "wrinkled;" it's withered. The point is that these people had nothing to show for their aging, just events. Nothing happened to them. Old women and old men should have wrinkles, and they should welcome them. They are signs of a life lived, the outward witness to a well-worn heart.

- the Lord looketh on the heart.

Book of Samuel

CHAPTER SIX

MOVING ON

**Some advice for your birthday:
Keep moving or they'll throw a tablecloth over you.**

Greeting card

I gave that card to my mother on her birthday a long time ago (she died in 1982), and I've been saying it ever since. It applies to me now. Fortunately, the media is full of advice to keep seniors moving, from tai chi and yoga, walking and dancing, to weight training and lessons in how not to fall. (I needed that one.)

My chapter title, "Moving On," suggests a goal, as opposed to getting a move on —mere activity— and goal infers purpose. A decision is involved, a choice has been made. By this time, I have made a lot of decisions. I seem to keep reaching crossroads. (Good metaphor.) We all do, for good or ill, scarcely aware of the far-reaching consequences. What about watershed moments? Not quite the same thing. Watershed offers the view from a height: back and down or forward and down. Crossroads offer more choices, at least three. The Latin word was *trivium,* meaning "place where three roads meet"— crossroads— protected by the female goddess, Hecate, often seen in triple form, known also by her Latin name, Trivia. Very serious.

Yet, now trivial means trifling, of little value or importance. From there it's an easy stretch (or sag) to trivializing, treating the problems of toddlers and old people lightly. Play Beanbag Toss with them to keep them moving.

I'm going to get an argument about the physical therapy that Beanbag Toss is good for and that the elderly need as they shuffle about their daily routine. It's just another example of what is being foisted on the old folks. Well, before they get to be old folks, they are elderly, before that, senior, before that, retired or shelved, and before that, aging, like, maybe 50. Life begins at 40; freedom begins at 55; so maybe 50 in the middle is the beginning of the end. For many men who are let go, that is, forcibly retired, at that age, it feels like the end. Too soon, it's not fair, it's too soon, people don't understand, they're wrong.

I was thinking about this in relation to travel, and I realized that most retirement homes, assisted living facilities, long-term care homes, nursing homes and elder hostels have a lot in common with tours, expeditions, excursions, outings and cruises. ElderTreks[40] are designed specifically for older wayfarers.

Years ago (1981), I took what I called my "Psycho Trip." It was the second of my investigative journalism projects for the *Toronto Star*. The first was my Old Lady Caper, to which I have already referred. I left home again and masqueraded as a former mental-health patient, checking into a boarding house close to Queen Street Hospital and its psychiatric ward. This time, I had to be more careful because all the occupants of the house were former psychiatric patients, controlled fairly well with prescription drugs and living close to the daycare facilities of the hospital and to a drop-in centre, a community club just for them. I asked a director

---

[40]   "ELDERTREKS is the world's first adventure travel company designed exclusively for people 50 and over. Established in 1987, ElderTreks offers active, off-the-beaten-path, small-group adventures by both land and sea in over 100 countries." (From the brochure, published annually.)

friend to teach me how to walk (with a shuffle and drooping shoulders) and to socialize with people (a contradiction actually), always averting my eyes, never looking anyone in the face, and to talk (simple words, incomplete sentences, unfinished thoughts). More stereotypes? But look closely. They all originate in fear. Life is difficult, hard to face head on.

I took an assumed name (my favourite cousin's so that I might respond to it readily—useful as it turned out) and asked my doctor to give me a prescription for tranquillizers in that name. I had it filled but never handed the pills in to the supervisor of the boarding house, who would dole out prescriptions at mealtimes to the boarders. The bottle of pills rattled convincingly in my purse and the name on it was my only ID. I carried a small amount of cash but mostly toilet paper. My roll was stolen from under my bed the first night. After that, I took paper from a public toilet every day and kept it in my purse.

I had to act all the time because, as I found out, I was being watched all the time. I couldn't be caught with pen and paper. I had a contact, Pat Capponi, herself a former patient who stayed on and served as an advocate and ombudsman for others trapped in defeat and despair, and who later became a published writer. I would check into her place every evening to write my report. Once, she let me wash my hair, but then I had to rub baby oil in it and mess it up because she said it looked too good.

This truly was a trip, a journey to a strange place in my own city, stranger even than the time I had spent as an old lady in a rooming house. That experience turned into a play[41] and so did this one, though, as with the other, I had not originally intended it. However, when I walked into the dining room, a dark basement room furnished with plain unmatched chairs and trestle tables, set properly by the residents and with a paper napkin at each place,

---

[41]   *A Place on Earth* is my most produced play all over the English-speaking world.

the lights went up for us to eat and for what I later thought of as the opening scene of a play. It was eerie. My housemates were very quiet, most of them drugged, very subdued and polite. They made conversation, as if they were fugitives from a Noel Coward play, but the conversation was somehow slightly skewed, a caricature of the originals, which I'm sure none of them had ever seen. Only now do I realize that what I witnessed was an adumbration of the future, of aging people's futures. They're neither mad nor incapacitated, but a lot of them are poor, weak, quiet, often helpless and too frequently on a premature journey to trivia—the crossroads.

So, which way are we going to go, if allowed, that is? No one is pushing for immortality, oh, except those people who like the idea of cryonics and pray for no power outages. I wonder if people who believe in immortality also believe in fairy tales. Do they think that it means you'll live forever in perfect health at about the age of 35 (everyone's ideal age)? Those people have not read the whole of *Gulliver's Travels* (1726). They think Jonathan Swift wrote about cute little people, the Lilliputians, later "immortalized" by whom else? Disney. If they've read more of the expurgated book, they know about the Brobdingnagians, giants who were much less warlike than the little guys. Few people today have gotten as far as Book III, to the country of Luggnagg, home of the Struldbrugs, the immortal people that Gulliver was looking forward to meeting and then was so disappointed when he did. They were immortal, but they were not ageless. They just kept on living and deteriorating, well past the Seven Ages of Man, condensed so succinctly by Shakespeare, and even his last stage is pretty depressing, the one "that ends this strange eventful history … mere oblivion, / Sans teeth, sans eyes, sans taste, sans everything."[42] The sad fact is that, given immortality or something like it, we might shuffle off this mortal coil gratefully, bored to death and even kind of thankful for Beanbag Toss.

---

[42]   From *As You Like It*.

What's so bad about living out our threescore years and ten, or whatever number we're up to now, just a full life without being too bored and with as little suffering as possible, all the while finding some meaning in the trip? Am I asking too much?

I suppose the answer depends on how much it costs. And there are no guarantees, no reprieve from boredom, no respite from the slings and arrows of outrageous fortune.

Years ago, when I first moved to Toronto from Stratford, I began exploring the lovely paths in the ravines in the city. One Sunday afternoon, totally disoriented (I have a terrible sense of direction), I stopped a man walking the other way and asked him, "Excuse me, but where am I?" And he said, "Where would you like to be?"

What a good answer!

Before you can figure out where you're going, you have to decide where you want to go. Before you can do that, you have to know who you are, or perhaps failing that, because that's pretty hard to figure out, then find out why you want to go anywhere. These are huge questions, life questions. If you want instant, glib answers, just go online. Google will lead you to all kinds of gurus who will tell you what to do and what to think, so many, in fact, that they make me wonder why I am struggling with these questions at all.[43]

Where am I going? Well, I've never been to me,[44] and neither have you, not yet, not enough. We move on. Keep moving.

Pussy cat, pussycat, where have you been?
James William Elliot (1833–1915), *National
Nursery Rhymes and Nursery Songs*

---

[43] See The *Book of Questions* in the bibliography
[44] "I've Never Been to Me" (1977) is the title of a song written and composed by Ron Miller and Kenneth Hirsch.

CHAPTER SEVEN

SEARCHING FOR SELF

We travel, initially, to lose ourselves,
and we travel, next, to find ourselves.
We travel to open our hearts and eyes.

Pico Iyer (b. 1957)

There are three trips a traveller takes: the first is to the destination; the second is to other people; and the third is the toughest: to one's self. All three involve discovery but the third most of all. I think that revelations are more interesting than mere information about accommodation, sights to be seen, miles covered, food, bargains, souvenirs or photography tips. It helps, though, if you have the odd adventure, the odder the better. For example:

I was taken hostage on a cruise a few years ago, before 9/11. Hostage! You think of strained, bruised faces, wincing in the harsh glare of camera lights as their owners try to assure their families that they are well and not being mistreated. It wasn't like that for us. I was one of 25 passengers and 14 staff members (our leaders and guides, the chef, the bartender and the cruise manager) trapped on the Russian ship LYUBOV ORLOVA when our Toronto-based tour company filed for bankruptcy, leaving their customers and staff high but not dry, forfeiting both goods and good will.

A Russian businessman (RB) owned the ship and needed cash for docking fees, fuel and salaries to bring his ship and crew home to the Black Sea. As the ship neared the Westman Islands off the coast of Iceland, our last scheduled visit before docking at Reykjavik, RB (who was not on board) issued an ultimatum: each of the passengers was to pay him 20,000 American dollars, cash, within 24 hours or the ship would sail to Gibraltar with all aboard. The demand was outrageous, and no one had that kind of money on hand. RB also demanded an equal amount from the tour company on shore. Not going to happen. So the ship turned south, revised destination Gibraltar. The minute it changed direction, against our express agreement, according to the law of the sea, we were officially kidnapped, taken hostage, and the poor Russian ship captain, in obeying his employer's orders, was breaking marine law. He was caught between a hard place and the Rock.

We were facing five days' hard sailing down the North Atlantic with the rumoured possibility that we would be dumped with our gear into two or three zodiacs, the rubber power boats used for wet landings. This would, however, have presented RB with another loss; each zodiac was worth about 15,000 dollars. Our "ordeal" was neither dramatic nor life threatening, but it was genuine. We were indeed prisoners, taken against our will, trapped by 100 fathoms of the icy North Atlantic. Some people were at risk, particularly those on necessary medication due to run out if they were compelled to stay away too long.

We had to have been among the most pampered hostages in history. The ship was fully stocked with delicious food and drink, enough for the cruise slated to follow ours as it went on to Greenland. The Russian crew continued to serve us: beds were made, meals were cooked, tables waited on, with an added bonus: an open bar. Once it was established that we were on our inexorable way, the tour bartender tore up the bar bills and broke out the champagne. Our "snack" on the penultimate day was smoked salmon with all the trimmings: dilled cream cheese, red onion and capers. Why not? The ship's contents would be going with the crew to Russia.

Unlike the food, information was sorely lacking, and we were unable to communicate with our families. Finally, we were permitted to send one monitored Fax message each, in order to make arrangements for what looked to be a longer trip than planned. People had to change their appointments and arrange for longer care for their children, their Alzheimer's relatives, dogs, plant-sitters, whatever. My message cost me 35 American dollars, but it never got through. (Funny how you remember numbers like that.)

The return flight arrangements were now obsolete. We had no idea how to deal with that. Our plans were completely up in the air, or I should say, all at sea. One of the Toronto staff had a satellite phone, and was thus able to bypass the ship's communications system. Through the phone and many sleepless hours, our guide was able to contact our respective embassies (Canadian and U.S.) and set up negotiations with RB who was eventually guaranteed payment on condition that his ship would drop us at the nearest city with an international airport. That would be Dublin, still a day and a half sailing time, time spent on our behalf arranging return flights.

Most of us spent a day in Dublin's fair city, sandwiched between two nights in a luxurious hotel. I had never been to Dublin, so it was a bonus. The anxiety we suffered may not have been for our lives, but some angst did arise from the extra unforeseen pinch on our pocketbooks. But we were alive, alive, oh!—and not as grateful as we should have been. I'm not sure I fully appreciated what had happened. I suffered some minor inconvenience; my travel plans were changed. I had planned to stay over in Reykjavik for a few days to visit a cousin. Instead, I got to see a bit of Ireland. But it made me think.

I started writing and making notes after that. Things, people and attitudes change. The world is growing smaller and more dangerous, and I am growing older and more vulnerable. There's a lot to rue and remember and also to relish and relive. As a seasoned traveller, you may have been everywhere, seen this, done that, but you probably haven't been to your self.

Often you don't know how you feel about a place or what you've learned until after you leave. Sometimes it takes a while to isolate the prevailing spirit (yours) from the country's. Forty-some years ago, I didn't realize how tense I was in iron-curtained Poland until we took off from Warsaw and I found myself breathing a heavy sigh of relief. A year after I toured Iceland for the first time in summer's almost perpetual daylight, I went back on the shortest day of the year to see for myself how cold and dark it could be. I remember best the endless dark winter in an old sod house, now a museum, and I continue to marvel at the illumination cast by the human spirits inhabiting it. This is one of the main reasons one travels, to distil the essence of a place and people, thereby discovering new sensations and reactions in one's self.

Everyone creates a private map of discovery. I remember when I went up the Jungfrau, standing outside the door of the shelter at the top of the sky with all the winds of the world blowing by, something happened in my brain. The wind swept clean a corner of it that will always remain wiped and empty and strangely peaceful.

The same thing happened when I viewed the Apsusiaajik Glacier near Greenland. We had been cruising slowly through a fog that remained reluctantly at bay, allowing us only sudden, unexpected visions, as gigantic icebergs hove into view through the murk. The fog swirled more thickly as we approached the glacier, and the boat slowed, but I could smell—land? No. Dulse, I guess. We were within 100 feet of the ice edge when the fog lifted and the sun came out over our right shoulders and lit up a massive wall of ice stretching from left to right in front of us for about the length of two football fields, enormous, majestic, sun-struck and awesome. And with the increasing awareness of Earth's changing climate, I know that those icebergs are not immutable. And I have become more immediately conscious of my mortality. I, too, will melt, thaw and resolve into a dew.[45]

One keeps searching and one keeps learning, marking new places on an internal map. It seems I had to go to Africa to ink upon my private map a fact about my own environment that I must have known all my life but had never recognized. Having tracked a pride of lions to their sleepy repletion after a rare giraffe kill, we gazed across a gully at a quartet of mourning giraffes silhouetted against a purple sky that promised rain. Our Great White Hunter, aka guide, made a simple comment:

"Each animal lives in its own environment."

Dead simple. For you, maybe. I never took biology or studied ecosystems. Today's Lesson:

All human creatures, though they live in or share the same country, or city, or house, or space, live in their own environment. The way I treat my living space affects theirs. As I say, dead simple. As one progresses, one learns. As a lightly seasoned traveller, I have learned a lot, and I am gradually filling in the blanks, seeing anew, doing something else, correcting illusions, adding facts, and realizing how much I am still missing in my quest. I still haven't been to me, not yet, not enough.

The funny thing is that I thought I knew who I was, and where I was in my Other Life—my busy, married life, when I had a husband and four children to look after and very little problem in defining myself. Then, suddenly, the definition changed. I was a widow, a single mother, the breadwinner, and I gradually left the

---

[45] *Hamlet.*

role I had taken for granted. Well, I didn't leave my post, as that had already happened, but I left the mind-set.

For a while, I was still married to a lifestyle. I still had a home and people to look after. My children were 12, 14, 16 and 18 when their father died, so they still needed care and attention. There were meals and laundry and seasons to be acknowledged. First the girls left, but I still had the boys at home and Matt, my youngest, needed extra time and care. It happened, though, that John, his older brother, moved into a university residence the same week that Matt was admitted into a special residential school, and suddenly I was totally alone. That's when I had my first identity crisis and started wondering what I was there for and what I was doing anyway. I described that feeling and a solution in my first book, *Beginnings: A Book for Widows* (1977):

"So often, since Bill died, I have asked myself in wonder, 'What am I doing here?' When I'm on a trip I know the answer.

"I'm visiting."

I suppose that's when I realized the value of travel. It defines you, if only in the simplest terms and sometimes only in negatives: I'm not at home. I'm not in my country. I'm not here. Oh, where am I then? Not then—now. Not here—elsewhere. Visiting. A stranger.

Somewhere along the road to re-definition, I left the middle class. I think others knew before I did that I no longer belonged in their midst. Our currency was not the same, not merely of money, of which I had a shortage, but of thoughts and conversation. I couldn't keep up with them, nor they with me. Time assumed different dimensions, too. I needed people most when they were busiest with their own lives, and I no longer had free time when they did because I was trying to make a living with my writing, of all things. (No one told me it couldn't be done.) The gap widened until I was no longer me, at least not the me I used to be.

At that same time I wrote a children's play, *The Old Woman and the Pedlar*,[46] based on the nursery rhyme about an old woman who is sleeping by the side of the road when a pedlar comes along and cuts her petticoats all round about.

"Lawk-a-mercy me," cries the old woman, "this is none of I," and she sets about trying to discover who she is if she is not herself. The whole play is a quest for identity. The old woman encounters different people on the road and asks for their help, to no avail. Finally, in despair, she gives up, saying that she's lost all hope.

With that, a sweet, adenoidal games-mistress type of creature arrives with a handful of balloons, asking if someone is calling her. Her name is Hope and she assures the old woman that she is never lost: "Abandoned sometimes, and dashed, but never lost." She asks the old woman what is wrong.

"You see," says the old woman, "I thought I knew who I was and where I was going."

"Who are you?" asks Hope. "And where are you going?"

My director pointed out to me that I was asking the same questions in *Beginnings*. That was a revelation. I may not have realized it, but I was already searching for self. It is, of course, a never-ending quest, but with any luck, I'll keep on making new discoveries.

This above all: to thine own self be true

William Shakespeare (1564–1616), *Hamlet*

---

46   First produced 1977, published 1978.

CHAPTER EIGHT

REMEMBERING

Twenty years from now you will be more disappointed by the things you didn't do than by the ones you did do. So throw off the bowlines, sail away from the safe harbor. Catch the trade winds in your sails. Explore. Dream. Discover

Mark Twain (1835–1910)47

The goal of exploration, dreaming and discovering is memory, the most precious thing a traveller can gather. One is warned, whether hiking on the Bruce Trail or exploring the Galapagos Islands, to leave nothing behind but footprints—and in the Galapagos you have to be careful where you leave those—but you are allowed to take away memories. I guess you're allowed to take pictures, too, easy these days with a multi-talented phone. I don't take pictures, so I never paid attention to that. Memories are something else, and I concede they are the reason people take

---

47   I read a note by a snarky blogger who claims that Mark Twain didn't say that, but he doesn't know who did. I didn't.

pictures, to help them remember. It never worked for my husband and me.

Years ago, in my Other Life, my husband decided he was going to take pictures on a trip we were taking to England. So he got a Leica and learned how to use it. Neither of us was big on cameras. Another time I might tell you what we did with our only movie camera.

The first picture he took was of a cantankerous swan that had taken up residence on a pond in a private park that Bill's uncle lived beside in Sussex. That was the only swan we were able to identify in the photos, and therefore the location, because it was single. After that, Bill took pictures of swans in groups on lakes or in parks or somewhere. Who knew? We came home with rolls of film and prints following (I told you this was years ago) of lovely, anonymous swans.

That's one of the reasons I don't take pictures. I live in the moment, enjoying swans or elephants or stingrays or scenery, taking a picture in my mind, later rerunning at random for sensations recollected in tranquility, as Dorothy Wordsworth and her brother used to say. And that is also why I write about the moments, about the trip to Shangri-La or Cousin Hebba's view from her living room (spectacular, especially at midnight in July overlooking Snaefelsness), or those tortoises breeding in a lagoon in the Galapagos Islands, or—but I digress.

I remember a trip I took to Newfoundland, not only the pictures but also the feelings that can't be photographed.

L'Anse aux Meadows had been on my bucket list for a long time, so when I saw that Adventure Canada was including it as a port-of-call on a circumnavigation of Newfoundland, I signed on. I must admit, I didn't pay much attention to what else was included in the trip. I had been to Newfoundland four or five times and thought I didn't need to know any more, arrogant creature that I am. I was wrong, I'm happy to say.

Rather than give you photographs, I'll give you a few images that have remained with me:

Leaving St. John's on the Clipper Adventurer, sailing clockwise, we arrived first at Fogo Island, which I knew nothing about. I can recall in great detail the aroma of a drying shed, which took me back to my Icelandic grandmother's back shed in Gimli, Manitoba, where she hung her hardfiskur—hardfish. I love hardfish. You break off a chunk, dip it in soft butter and chew. Bill used to say it tasted like old toenails, and I asked him how he knew what old toenails tasted like.

I also remember the lovely "lunch" the local ladies prepared for us. We were confused about what a lunch was. They call it a snack; to us that first day it was more like dinner: all kinds of delicious fish dishes plus the island treat—tarts filled with bakeapples (sic), also called cloud berries, which are golden yellow, filled with seeds and enhanced with lots of sugar.

And then there were the stark, amazing lines of the artists' residences designed by contemporary architects, seemingly out of place among the comfortable conventional houses common to a fishing village, but suited to the environment of sea and rocks and sky. These buildings are like the residences in the Leighton Artists' Colony in the Banff Centre (Canada) in that they are dedicated to the creative use by artists who come to dream and write or paint. They're not really residences (one would have trouble living in one), but they are palaces of the imagination.

L'Anse aux Meadows was the second stop on the cruise. The re-created site was the briefly inhabited settlement of Leif the Lucky, son of Eirik the Red, occupied, but not permanently, over a period of three or four years. As you may or may not know, my maternal grandparents came separately from Iceland during the great exodus after Hecla erupted; they met and married in Winnipeg and moved up to Gimli to raise their family. My grandfather's store, founded in 1899, is the only general store in Canada still being run by the same family, fourth generation, by my cousins with whom I share that grandfather. Like most Icelanders, or Western Icelanders as we are called by those still living in Iceland, I'm a nut about genealogy and our provenance. It was, therefore, natural for me to want to seek out L'Anse aux Meadows, site of the first discovery of North America 4 centuries before Columbus.

It was a wet, foggy day; we were delayed in our landing because of the fog. I didn't mind that, nor did I mind being cold because it was all the more comforting to go inside the main longhouse and enjoy the fire and the bannock (fried bread) offered with a dip of bakeapple jam. You can take a photograph, as most people did, but you can't take a picture of the warmth of my emotions. I guess an experience like that is the closest we can get to a time machine.

After that, I thought the rest of the trip was gratuitous. I didn't know what to expect and was quite willing to go along with it. I was also willing to forgive myself if I was not physically up to the demands of the excursions. As it turned out, that was not a problem. The leaders running that cruise were very tolerant. They arranged each stop with different levels of energy and stamina, that is, age, in mind. We could choose long, medium or short walks, and cars were arranged in many places, supplied by local inhabitants, along with the food.

So how do you photograph the taste of blueberry wine, or of *toutons* (a different version of fried bread, offered with molasses or maple syrup)? I didn't need pictures; I just needed taste buds, pen and paper and a good memory.

On one of the last mornings, we didn't walk at all. We were taken in zodiacs up a long, broad, beautiful fjord with magnificent rock walls soaring up from the water. The Zodiac driver was conscientious and generous in his treatment of the photographers, circling and closing in and pointing out good shots. I just sat and gazed. I mean, it was like the swans. When you take the rocks home, where are you? And does it matter? I was there, in the moment. Gradually, all the rocks and water have melded and blended into a composite picture of all the beauty spots of this Earth I have so far been privileged to behold. This is not a "been-there-done-that" attitude. It's "here I am in the now and so grateful for the moment."

By the time one is old and grey, one swan is much like another, but memories are not. For those who are losing their memory and other things, apparently short-term memory is the first to go, which is a kind of inverse blessing because long-term memory is a comfort and a joy. Have you ever noticed that you can't reproduce pain from memory? You can remember when you were in pain and what caused it, but you can't feel it. But you can reproduce pleasure and laughter with the aid of memory. You can find yourself chuckling at something that tickled your fancy years ago, or smiling at the antics of a child long grown to adulthood, or feeling pride and pleasure in some past achievement. That's the paradoxical blessing of memory. It remains, fresh and welcome. Remembered laughter is present laughter.

As for the first half of Twain's (or someone's) encouragement, that you'll be disappointed by the things you didn't do, my father used to say you won't remember the cost of something you did, but you'll remember the regret if you didn't do it. I've thought of that often, as when I wafted up over a dark jungle in a 7-passenger balloon (well, 6 plus the balloonist), rising with the sun above the backs of eagles and elephants, in spite of my fear of heights. I paid extra for it, but I don't remember how much. I also paid extra to fly in a 10-passenger plane from Milford Sound back over the Southern Alps to Queenstown instead of taking the bus. I had a great view of the Milford Track from the air.

Why do I keep going so high? I must admit that the older I get, the less I feel like rocketing up a mountain. I have the memory of a view, but I'm grateful not to be able to reproduce the apprehension or the discomfort. Inertia has become attractive and comfortable. The English poet Philip Larkin (1922–1985) said he wouldn't mind seeing China if he could come back home the same day. There's a lot to be said for being at home and staying there. Perhaps that is part of getting ready for a trip, not just getting ready to go but getting ready to settle. It's nice to look forward to the next adventures, and I still have a few in mind, but it's also nice to stay put. I give more than a nod to creature comforts now. It's cheaper not to go, too. I'm actually quite pleased now to cross out places that used to be on my agenda. Again, it's not "been there, done that," it's "I don't have to go there." I have shrunk my bucket list with equanimity.

"We'll always have Paris." That line from the movie *Casablanca* (1942) is a cliché now, and you can fill in the name of any place that is significant to you with the assurance that your audience will know what you mean. It's called an allusion. It's also an illusion—memory, that is—the riveting power of total recall that nails your heart in place. You may not remember where you put your car keys, but some things you don't forget.

If you're old enough or lucky enough to have friends or family to celebrate an astronomical number of your life's years, then you'll know that people are asked for their presence, not presents. Often, however, they are charged with bringing along a reminiscence, some memory of a shared past. Or perhaps you have been invited to do it for someone else, a contemporary with whom you go a long way back. You can embroider, but you can't lie. Don't panic. Just start slowly with "I remember …" It'll come to you. That's what age is good for if you're lucky: long, clear memories, the best baggage you can take with you and bring home, whether it's to a party or from a trip.

This is memoir at its most basic. Memoirs are very popular these days, and they are overdone. There's a difference between a memoir and an autobiography. A memoir is selective, often random, and not exhaustive. An autobiography is a blow-by-blow account of a life and is usually documented with dates and facts and authentication, but it can be fictionalized (and often is). Young celebrities still in their teens are publishing what they call their memoirs, though they have short lives to remember, while older ones are bringing them out in successive tell-all volumes. A memoir can be a simple reminiscence called up for the sake of a friend or a more detailed account for the sake of family or grandchildren who want to know what it was like in the olden days. Family trees are useful, too, for genealogical or medical reasons. This is all part of getting ready for the big examination at the end. Clean your house! Leave nothing but memories.

I like the title the American writer Gore Vidal (1925–2012) gave to his memoir/autobiography: *Palimpsest.*."[48] It comes from the ancient Romans who used wax tablets on which to write (scratch) and which could be quite easily erased for new material. Later documents (papyrus, vellum), were less and less easily erased, and the methods of erasure were more effective until today when it is possible to recover deleted files from a computer hard drive. Vidal's word for his memoir was apt. As long as one keeps writing, the story changes, doesn't it? For the writer, it pays to have a short (erasable?) memory, if one is still in the process of inventing oneself.

But the thought of memory draws up other considerations, especially as one grows older. One's own memory bank can become a palimpsest, and the material is not so easily recovered from one's brain. Anxious caregivers arm their loved ones with memory boards to enable them to find their way home.

The British writer Tony Judt (1948–2010), who ended his life in New York, dying of amyotrophic lateral sclerosis,[49] created a memoir, *The Memory Chalet*, conceived and memorized during his sleepless nights and repeated to an assistant each morning for a written record. It's a memoir of his life and also a guide for dying.

---

[48] In textual studies, a palimpsest is a manuscript page, either from a scroll or a book, from which the text has been scraped or washed off so that the page can be reused for another document. *Wikipedia*

[49] ALS, commonly referred to as "Lou Gehrig's disease."

Other writers have used the night for such "writing." The poet John Milton (1608–1674) comes to mind. I remember learning that he dictated what he created during the night. (Let's hear it for the amanuensis!) I looked into this story and found that a number of paintings by different artists have dealt with this subject: poor old blind Milton with his eyes blunk out, reciting *Paradise Lost* to his long-suffering daughters, who caught his immortal words. I'll name three of the artists, but there were more: George Romney (1741–1825), Henry Fuseli (1741–1825), and Eugène Delacroix (1980–1863).

I guess it was one way of being immortalized. These days, in a so-called paperless society (hah!), it's almost impossible to be ignored or forgotten. Big Brother and Facebook are watching you.

I remember thinking defensively, when I heard of that act of creation— holding what one had "written" in one's head until it could be dictated and recorded— that Milton didn't have to remember phone numbers or anniversaries or birthdays the way I did. And now, passwords! I go crazy with passwords. When I think of the time lost trying to remember them or to replace a forgotten one, it's enough to turn me into a Luddite.

Time-motion studies have been conducted measuring the amount of time and energy lost in looking for lost keys or eyeglasses or whatever else elderly or absent-minded people mislay. There are courses to help them improve, ways of recovering lost things. I think of poor Miss Prism in Wilde's *The Importance of Being Earnest* (1895) who seriously mislaid a manuscript. It has been proved that stress damages memory.

The key to a good memory is to remember in the first place. Attention must be paid. The item to be remembered must be defined and cemented. One must lay down a "neural pathway" so that the way may be retraced. There are, of course, mnemonics, to aid in the recovery. Anyone who studied music—well, anyone my age— can remember the aide-memoire "Every Good Boy Deserves Fudge."[50] The initials stand for the notes in the treble clef.

I read that the human mind can handle only seven new ideas at one time. The good news is that they are channeled into different areas for storage—that is, different areas of the brain to accommodate, for example, faces, numbers, skills, first and second language (routed to different areas), and so on. The best advice I read to cope with all this is to sleep on it. It works.

Good nutrition is very popular these days, not just for health and longevity but also for brain activity. Pick up any newspaper or magazine and you'll get lots of advice on what you should eat for a good memory. Among other things: blueberries! I like blueberries, but you can look up other foods that will help you to remember birthdays, anniversaries, passwords, directions and where you put your glasses. I prefer built-in mnemonics rather than prosthetic ones, but these days most people rely on external hard drives of one sort or another, that is, on a good retrieval system, preferably digital. Woe to those who lose their data.

I still love paper. I am very blessed in that the University of Manitoba, my alma mater, relieves me of my paper files and stores them in their archives. Better there than in my home. The first time I sent out an offering of my past, in some 30 boxes, they told me that I had included 3 acorns and a dead mouse. Not intentionally. That dated from when I still lived up north on a lake in Muskoka. I guess you could call that a by-product of my memory cache.

I'm grateful that I still have good long-term memories in the hard drive in my head. I guess, like good legs, memories are the last to go. I hope so.

Memory is the diary that we all carry about with us.

Oscar Wilde (1854–1900)

---

[50]   The mnemonic is still used today. I checked.

CHAPTER NINE

FORGETTING

To forgive is wisdom, to forget is genius.

Joyce Cary (1888–1957)

I had a friend whose mother, whenever they had an argument, would recall in detail every single thing her grandchildren had broken. She seemed to gloat as the list grew. My mother, bless her, though we had our differences, never did that. When one of my children broke something in her house, she'd say, "Good! That's one less thing to dust," and forgot about it.

This is not about remembering; this is about forgetting. We worry a lot these days about forgetfulness. Even relatively young women (especially women) worry when they forget a name, less frequently an engagement, sometimes where the car keys are, and often whether or not they turned off the stove. Most of us, when we commit a minor sin of omission like this, worry about Old Timers' Disease or apologize for a "senior moment." I blame my internal Rolodex file for getting rusty or overloaded. Mild and infrequent lapses like those listed are not early warning signs of incipient Alzheimer's or dementia or senility. They happen to all of us, sometimes exacerbated by lack of sleep, or stress or a hangover.

As always, there are different ways to approach the problem of forgetfulness, just as there are different kinds of absent-mindedness. Of course, everyone has things they tend to forget regularly (accidentally on purpose?), like husbands forgetting anniversaries, or wives forgetting the price of a new dress. But these are stereotypes. I have a friend who puts up little signposts to remind her to take her vitamin pills every day. Another one has a Post-it Note on her car dashboard reminding her not to turn left on such-and-such a street between 4 and 6 p.m. She has had two expensive tickets for doing so and does not want another one.

Fridge doors and magnets were invented for forgetful people. Everybody's favourite bulletin board bristles with appointments and recipes and photographs (delightful reminders of lovable people) and grocery lists. We take calendars and clocks for granted until the day we see a loved one get confused about the date and time. It seems we all need mnemonics, but most of us are still a long way from memory boards.

I had the sorrow and privilege of seeing a close friend develop Parkinson's disease and Alzheimer's (they often go together) as he fumbled his way out of life. We had been friends in our home city (Winnipeg) since our teens. We were both married, to other people, and ended up in Ontario. My husband and he had been fraternity brothers, rather competitive, I gather, but friends. We saw the couple once or twice a year. After Bill died, I had major surgery for bleeding ulcers[51] and they visited me in hospital (not many people did). When I moved into Toronto, Ralph (not his real name) and his wife helped me. Later, I moved to Muskoka and lost touch. But when Ralph's wife died, some dozen years later, he called me, asking for help in getting tickets for some Stratford plays. Thus began a culturally oriented twilight friendship.

---

[51] I had 5/8 of my stomach removed. That was customary then, a year or so before a pill was discovered that eliminated the need for a knife.

He asked me to live with him, and I demurred. However, we agreed to be companions for travel and theatre and other events. After all those years, I thought I knew him very well, though of course we had not lived together. I began to notice little things, quite charming errors at first. He referred to the Welland Canal as "that man-made ditch." I could overlook small oversights on his part: mistaking a meeting time, not showing up for dinner when invited, forgetting to bring a promised bottle of wine, or for not returning something he had borrowed, and oh, yes, forgetting my birthday. I thought at first that he was careless or had been so spoiled by his wife that he took things for granted. Someone else had probably covered for his careless lapses. Then he forgot his passport for a trip outside the country. It cost him a lot of money and me a lot of anxiety for a cabbie to help him retrieve the document from his home, located in a distant suburb, in time to catch the plane. I stopped driving with him because he didn't seem to notice traffic or stop signs, and I was almost killed once when he ignored a car driving right at us, my side. I screamed and someone swerved and I vowed never again.

Then he was diagnosed, and it seemed to be a signal for swift deterioration to take place, though, in fact, it was not that swift. A couple of years passed with home help—and me—before his family put him in a beautifully appointed facility with, I think it was called, a Reminiscence Floor, something like that, out of the city. I took a Go train once a week to visit him, though, as time passed, I'm not sure if he knew me. I felt I could not abandon him.

I talked a lot, recalling old friends and days in Winnipeg, chatting as if we were old friends, which we were. His speech had deteriorated to grunts and his gestures to involuntary waving about. But once in a while, after I'd told him a story about someone we knew, he would say, clear as a bell:

"I didn't know that."

I heard a song a long time ago, the message being something to the effect that "folks don't touch old people anymore."

Remembering that, I made a point every week when I left Ralph, to stroke his temples and face and to drop a kiss lightly on his forehead. He always said "Thank you." Someone was still in there, somewhere.

We are more aware of and apprehensive about Alzheimer's now, and a lot more is being said and written and studied about it. It was just happenstance that I learned about it firsthand, not quite as emotionally hard-hit as if it had been my husband afflicted with it, but close enough to touch me. Whether it's you or I who may develop it or someone close to us, it's the caregiver who has to live through the dying fall.

Lisa Genova (b.1970) is an American neuroscientist and writer. She self-published her first novel, *Still Alice* (2009), about a Harvard professor who suffers early onset Alzheimer's and who tells her story in the first-person as she declines. The book was a best seller, translated and sold in 30 countries around the world. A movie based on it, starring Julianne Moore, was released in 2015 and won an Oscar for its star. I read it in one gulp. Ralph didn't want to read it while he still could. I don't blame him.

That's the hardest part about forgetting, the inconceivable thought of losing one's Self.

There are other causes and reasons for forgetting, some as disturbing as the losses implicit in Alzheimer's, for different reasons. Some are public, like a state's eradication of a previous hero by removing commemorative plaques and statues from public display and consequent private memory. Then there is the deliberate, collective forgetting of a national shame, like the invaders' past treatment of indigenous people or, on a smaller scale, a college's refusal to acknowledge female sexual harassment on its campus. Only recently has there been an attempt at reconciliation or reparation.

People forget on an even smaller scale, but it's just as overwhelming in its effectiveness. After a sex change, the individual and his/her co-operative family and friends forget her/his former identity.

Some people forget people who are not convenient or useful to them to know. I had a friend who said once, proudly, "I don't know anyone I don't like." At first that sounds broad-minded and tolerant, but he meant that he had written them off; he simply did not know them, ever.

I've already referred to my overloaded Rolodex file. It's a metaphor for my mind. I simply discard useless-to-me information to lighten the load, bearing in mind the rule that states how soon you'll need something you get rid of. One does need a good retrieval system. There's always Wikipedia.

Then there's a kind of forgetting that's becoming more common in our disposable consumer society. We buy things, small appliances mostly, or so it seems to me, that will break or be obsolete far too soon, and we'll have to buy more, ignoring or forgetting their short life span. I have one friend, my age, married only a year after me, who still owns and operates the Sunbeam pop-up toaster she received as a wedding present. All of her friends, including me, find that incredible. Her husband is gone, may he rest in peace, but her toaster lives on.

The rest of us keep on buying things that will wear out sooner than later, at which time we will buy more, new, shoddy, short-lived products. That's what keeps the economy going.

Another common habit of forgetting also happens to everyone, sooner or later. In English we call it a "Tip of the Tongue," or TOT. The need for a word or name arises during a casual conversation, but it doesn't pop up. It just lies there, on the tip of the tongue. Usually, the forgetful one gets a little agitated because the first letter comes to mind or a rough definition or association. The feeling is that retrieval is on its way, on the tip of the tongue. But it doesn't come. I've mentioned elsewhere that it took me two days to remember the words for walrus ivory carving. Such a relief when the correct answer pops up!

I don't have quite the same problem with voices. I may see an actor, a supporting character, not a well-known star, on television, and the voice is familiar. Not the face. I can't remember faces, but I'm pretty good at voices. So an actor's face is no help when I am trying to recall a name; in any case, the make-up or context is different and provides no clues. However, I can often identify the voice. Score one for me. That is, if you're keeping score. At my age, who's counting?

I should, though, count or keep track. When we first moved to Stratford, people had parties for us because they wanted to meet the new manager of the Stratford Festival and his wife. At one of these affairs, I went up to a woman and said, "Hello, I'm Betty Jane Wylie," and she said, "That's the third time this week you've told me that."

It got worse. I mean it happened frequently, but I simply cite one of the more embarrassing moments. I sold a book to a new-to-me publisher and I had lunch with the publisher and the managing editor to discuss the contract. Later that week, I went into the publishing office and met a woman in the hall. I said I had phoned Ms. So-and-So and was here to talk to her. "I am Ms. So-and-So," said the woman. Oops!

The oops! factor is always painful. We want to forget incidents when we behaved badly or made a boo-boo or caused another's embarrassment, if not our own. These are the faux pas that rise up to taunt us during wakeful nights. I don't have to remind you what they are. Everyone has such niggling, painful reminders of their own shortcomings. I remember a character in an Aldous Huxley novel who suffered from this kind of recollection she would rather have lost. Huxley called such memories "floaters."

Miss Thriplow in *Those Barren Leaves* (1925) recalls a floater and is "overcome by a feeling of self-reproach and retrospective shame." That's probably all I can safely quote without breaking copyright rules. The commonest floater is the one that lies there when you have put your foot in your mouth, like asking after a person's mother who has just died a few weeks before and you should have remembered. Or saying how much you hate rhyming verse, especially in narrative form, and your friend has just published a whole book of it as a novel. You will be able to add many examples, I'm sure, if not now, then tonight, when some tactless bumble of yours floats up to torment you. They are not innocent errors; they are things you should have known better than to say or do. What were you thinking of? Well, actually, you weren't thinking at all.

Anyway, such gaffes encourage a kind of forgetfulness we all welcome. Too good a memory makes us feel guilty about forgetting, like birthdays, appointments and names, to say nothing of promises and debts. We are all remorseful at our lapses, depending on the significance of what has been forgotten. That's when "if only" becomes a painful cry and not a rueful sigh. And that's when we start worrying about Alzheimer's and other organic causes of forgetting and asking ourselves when it will happen to us.

I think the hazards of the forgetful brain worry us more than any other aspect of aging. We're more worried about getting through the day safely and efficiently than we are about snubbing our friends or forgetting the rules of bridge. (I never could learn them.) One day, several years ago, I forgot how to make gravy, and I was astonished. I mean, how could I forget? Well, I could forget because I hadn't made it for a long time and my mind had long since rejected gravy as too fattening to be worth remembering. I've made it since, on occasion, and it was okay. It's like riding a bicycle. That's another skill it's said you'll never forget.

I remember I had an ear infection and went to the doctor for a diagnosis and prescription, and I asked him if I could swim, and he said, "I don't know. Could you swim before?" A comedian! But the question is valid. If you knew something once, if it was sufficiently encoded, that is, if it registered the first time, it should still be there—somewhere. Can you still balance a chequebook? I can't, but then I never could.

Scientists used to believe that the brain stops developing and learning after a certain age, but it's evident now to them, and to us aging laypeople, that we can keep on learning.

Canadian psychiatrist and psychoanalyst Dr. Norman Doidge describes an astonishing new science called neuroplasticity. His book *The Brain That Changes Itself: Stories of Personal Triumph from The Frontiers of Brain Science* (2007), challenges the idea that the human brain locks in after a certain age and can't be changed, that is, that it's incapable of learning anything new or developing new patterns.

"Ruts" they used to be called. Stuck in a rut, welded to old habits, unable to change or grow, we thought. However, Doidge informs us that brains can open new paths of behaviour, even in advanced years.

I read his book when I began to study Icelandic. It's a difficult language because it still declines and conjugates and has changeable articles that must agree with the gender of the thing they refer to. I found myself fondly and ruefully recalling my student days when I studied Latin and Greek. The rules came easily then. But I'm attempting a good thing now, good for me.

A cohort of Dr. Doidge's, American neuroscientist Dr. Michael Merzenich[52] is a dazzling pioneer studying age-related cognitive decline. He formed a new company, Posit Science, developing brain exercises to enable new events to register in our nervous system. Aging people may seem competent enough, but they are simply replaying mastered skills. They—we—must learn new ones. "That's why," says Dr. Merzenich, "learning a new language in old age is so good for improving and maintaining the memory generally ... You will gradually sharpen *everything* up again and that will be very highly beneficial to you."[53]

---

[52] Also called Merz; the Good Doctor; the Brain Guy,

[53] Michael Merzenich, quoted by Norman Doidge in Doidge's book, *The Brain That Changes Itself,* p. 87.

I guess I have my mother to thank for the opportunity to learn Icelandic in my later life. She wouldn't let me learn the language as a child because she wanted to gossip with her sisters and mother without my understanding. Still, the few hints I remember from my grandmother have been helpful.

Merz's game, Posit Science, has exercises for remembering words and language using games from Fast ForWord (sic), designed to help the brain retain or retrain its plasticity. The games are aimed at different processes: auditory or visual.

When my challenged son, Matt,[54] was a little boy, barely into kindergarten (he started late), I played games with him at home to encourage his auditory and visual processing and kept on as he progressed into something approximating elementary grades. I learned what to do from books and from a wonderful speech therapist named Judy Ball, who took him under her wing and lent me some equipment when I could not reproduce the exercises at home.

I digress, I know, but it's strange—or is it merely coincidental?—that exercises initially designed to stimulate a challenged young brain are being developed now to improve an aging one. I think I was ahead of Lumosity, but I'm going to get an argument.

Lumosity, considered a game, is an online brain training and neuroscience research company based in San Francisco, California. Founded in 2005 and launched in 2007, it offers more than 40 games designed to improve the player's brain in the areas of memory, attention, flexibility, speed of processing and problem solving.

I have two friends who subscribe to Lumosity, with differing attitudes to it. The one challenged my belief that earning a new language was as good as Lumosity. She plays regularly and claims it has improved her brain. The other friend, also a woman, enjoys

---

54   I've written a book about him, *The Book of Matthew*, McLelland and Stuart 1984.

it but thinks she has merely become better at playing. I asked her assessment of it/them and this is what she wrote:

"I am thinking a little more about my time with Lumosity, and overall I do actually find most of the games fun, with some being far more challenging than others to the point that I get tense. I began testing myself daily but am down to sometimes twice a week. The main reason I started Lumosity training was due to its almost guaranteed assurances of 'cognitive improvements.' My scores have improved hugely, but I'm not convinced that translates into cognitive improvement, but rather that I am getting better at the particular tests."

This is all kind of mechanical, though. We're treating the brain like another muscle of the body that needs to be exercised in order to function well, and that's a good thing. But we remember with the heart as well as with the brain.

That seems suspiciously poetic. Did I really write that? I believe it, but did I say it? No, I didn't.

It's an idea that has become part of the lore surrounding Alzheimer's disease. It comes from Malaysian writer Tan Twan Eng (b.1972), whose first novel was long-listed for the Man Booker Prize in 2007, and whose second novel was short-listed in 2012 and won the Asia Man Prize. I looked up his quotes with their words of soft, palatable wisdom that reminded me of Kahlil Gibran (*The Prophet*). Although I had never heard of the novelist or read anything of his, I must have absorbed his perceptions:[55]

The mind forgets, but the heart will always remember. And what is the heart's memory but love itself?

Tan Twan Eng (b.1972)

---

[55] How can copyright ever be safe in this porous world?

CHAPTER TEN

CAREGIVING

I'll grow old and shout at them from a wheelchair. That's what they're waiting for. They get their own back for all the years I bullied them. They wheel you where they like. "Take me there." "You went there yesterday. We want to go the other way." "Take me down to the beach, I want to see the sea. "You don't want to see the sea. You saw the sea yesterday. The wind's bad for your head. If you misbehave and catch a cold we'll shut you up in bed. You'll stay there for good this time."

Mrs. Rafi[56]

According to the World Health Organization (WHO), the number of older people in developing countries who are no longer able to look after themselves is forecast to quadruple by 2050, reaching an astounding 350 million and outnumbering all children under the age of 14. "Many of the very old lose their ability to live independently because of limited mobility, frailty or other physical or mental health problems. Many require some form of

---

[56]   Mrs. Rafi is a character in Edward Bond's play The Sea (1973).

long-term care, which can include home nursing community care and assisted living residential care and long stays in hospitals."[57]

Nowadays more children than ever before will know their grandparents, and even their great-grandparents. I just wish my grandchildren would hurry up and include me in that awesome statistic.[58]

We know that the boomer generation has contributed to that surge. The first Boomers started receiving their OAS cheques (Old Age Security, issued at age 65) in 2010. They are the so-called Sandwich Generation with aging parents, still living but newly dependent and needing help, and also with grown children, sort of independent but not yet self-supporting and needing help. It's a financial and a physical squeeze. The catch is that the Boomers have fewer children, hence, fewer guarantees of support when they reach old age.

Carol Abaya, an American journalist nationally recognized as the expert on the so-called Sandwich Generation, has added a couple of additional descriptions to the original epithet: the Club Sandwich and the Open-Face. The Club filling comprises those in their 50s and 60s, i.e., Boomers, with a bottom layer, that is, grandchildren, added to the grandparents who are the upper side (not upper crust), also Boomers with very young children, plus aging parents plus grandparents. Abaya identifies the Open-Face as anyone else involved in caregiving of the elderly. However you look at it, it makes for a squeezed filling.

When I was writing my books about family,[59] the catch phrase then was "empty nest syndrome," referring to the feelings of loss and a kind of bereavement that parents, especially women, were supposed to experience when the last child leaves home: for

---

[57] World Health Day release, 2012.
[58] *Flash!* They did! I have a great-granddaughter and a great-grandson now.
[59] *All in the Family,* Key Porter Books, 1988; *Family: An Exploration,* Northstone Books, 1997.

college, travel, job, marriage, whatever. These days, the joke is that the older generation can hardly wait to claim the bedrooms and storage space for themselves. However, they are discovering that their eagerness and relief are a mite premature. I changed the phrase "empty nest." I called it the "revolving nest" because the kids kept coming home again. Divorce, unemployment, despair and other trauma sent them back with their tails and high hopes between their legs. And then there was a "failure to launch", recognized in a rom-com (2006) by that name, about a not-so-young man who found his childhood home and his mother's cooking and laundry service preferable to his own efforts.

I've been around long enough to have seen and lived part of all this; I helped cause the boomer generation, and I experienced the revolving nest. Bill and I were living in a rented duplex with two very young children (almost 3 and 18 months) when we tried to buy a house. The house, though new and never occupied, was not eligible for a new house mortgage. We had already given notice when we received this news, and we had to vacate our rented duplex by the end of the month. My parents took us in while the new house, mortgage approved, was being built. I reverted to childhood, or almost. I didn't hang my towels on the floor, but I seemed to have lost all sense of responsibility for simple household management or meal planning. It must have driven my mother crazy, witnessing such a role reversal in an adult child. Imagine how poignant it must be when the reversal is the result of an illness, frailty or dementia in a parent who has always been the authority figure.

Well, we're all caregivers, one way or another. My youngest child (adult now), as I've already reported, has always needed extra care. Care is different for young children, or even adult ones, than it is for elderly parents, because with the younger generation, you are usually expecting growth and increasing independence while with the older recipient you are simply trying to maintain an acceptable quality of life with no anticipation of a return to former strengths. This is not always true with a challenged person. It takes a lot of care (patience, repetition, tolerance, humour and persistence) to enable him to take adequate care of himself.

My aim for Matthew was always to help him achieve independence, to have a life, work and a home of his own, without too much reliance on his siblings. I wanted him to be a welcome guest in their homes and not a burden they reluctantly put up with. We have been fortunate. I worked hard to make that happen for Matt, but I couldn't have done it without government and community assistance. For example, Loblaw's provides jobs for people like Matt. It's not a "sheltered" job. He earns his salary, albeit low, but with allowance within it for increases, as a buggy gopher. He has recently been awarded a 25-year service pin. I told him that's as good as my Order of Canada because it means he showed up for work every day, reliable and productive. Not without a little help from his friends, including Bonnie, his current social worker provided by Community Living Toronto, who checks up on him and his assigned apartment mate every week to make sure the two men are functioning well. That is, they are doing their laundry, banking, cooking and shopping and (very little) cleaning. I remember thinking that Matt's older brother and his roommates could have used such a check when they were undergraduates sharing a house while they attended university. John used to say as he walked past a sink full of dirty dishes, "Someone has to wash that or feed it."

Caregiving takes many forms. It takes a village, and we are blessed in this age and on this continent to have such villages.

I've been reading a number of books by caregivers: devoted or not daughters or sons who have reported on the hazards, pitfalls, pains and rewards of caring for an aging parent. I didn't go through this experience to any extent. Both my parents were very efficient in their passing. My father was diagnosed with cancer of the liver at a time before liver transplants and given an accurate estimate of about 3 months to live. He stayed at home as long as he could—till the last weekend—enabled by my mother and her sister, his caregivers. Matthew was in nursery school twice a week by then, and on those mornings, I went to see my father and act as amanuensis. To begin, I made him tell me my favourite story from my childhood about the time he went to help Santa Claus when he had the flu.

Jack—he preferred to be called Jack after he deemed me too old to call him Daddy—also told stories of Winnipeg in his early days, identifying streets with changed names and houses or buildings with interesting histories. I wrote down and sold all his stories to the Winnipeg Free Press. They were run on successive Saturdays until the morning before his death (on his 66th birthday). He roused himself to look at the Saturday feature, so pleased still to be paid for something he had done. That was my caregiver's gift to him.

My mother was even more efficient in her departure. I had moved her from Winnipeg to Toronto to live near me in a studio apartment down the hall after she had suffered several small "implosions," mini-strokes that left her with no memory of some lapsed time—sometimes on the floor. I stocked her with food for daytime needs, had her for dinner every night, shared my newspaper and cleaning lady with her and did her laundry. It was pretty perfunctory. After Bill died, I was busy fighting for my financial survival, trying to make a living for my family and me. So I wasn't much of a caregiver. I realized later that I never took Mom to the hairdresser or to the movies. She never complained, not for the 5 months she was with me. At least I was there. One night she called, saying that she was "uncomfortable." (She had a very high pain threshold.) I did what I could for her until I realized that I had to check her into a hospital because I really couldn't cope. Emergency surgery revealed an embolism that had destroyed her small intestine to the point of no return (gangrene). She was sewn up and did not wake up from the anesthetic. I said the 23rd Psalm to her, as I had done for my father.

How privileged am I to have been present at the departures of my parents and my husband? Talk about closure! Painful, though.

Once you have tried to help those close to you, and suffered along with them, you try to pass on your expertise to others. It's called "paying it forward" now, and it goes on every day, not only in organized volunteer work but also in daily acts of service.[60] I share my cooking with a number of my apartment neighbours, who may vary from week to week according to their needs. I am grateful to offer soup because there's no such thing as a small pot of soup. My line is "good soup makes good neighbours."[61] I also bake muffins for people who need them. Who doesn't need a muffin?

My brother spent the last several years of his life in a Baha'i home for the elderly in Nanaimo. I went to visit him 2 or 3 times, staying for supper and renting a spare room for the night. As we were all gathering for dinner, I saw Jack (named after his father) carefully folding a number of napkins and placing them at one of the places at our table. He explained that these were for one of our tablemates who had trouble with her eating and swallowing and who needed extra equipment to help her mop up.[62] After dinner, he would escort her back to her room in a very courtly manner. I saw him do this each time I visited him.

"Jack," I said the first time, "you are a saint."

"I try to be," he said simply.

A saint *and* a caregiver.

---

[60] "You don't pay love back, you pay it forward." An old concept presented in a book, *In the Garden of* Delight (1916), by Lily Hardy Hammond (1859-1925). *Pay It Forward* was a movie made in 2000, based on the novel by Catherine Ryan Hyde.

[61] Modifying Robert Frost's words: "Good fences make good neighbors."

[62] I've used this in a recent screenplay I'm working on. To a writer, everything is grist for the mill.

I'll tell you what caregivers need a lot of, and that's patience. When Matt was little and needed to learn everything the hard way, I needed a lot of patience. His speech therapist, Judy Ball, provided extra patience along with some technical assistance. Audio aids are taken for granted now, and everyone has access to them. I had a tinny little tape player that I played nursery rhymes and songs on for Matt. I began to use it to help him develop his focus and attention span. For this I needed two tape decks: one with a story or song on it and another one for me to record that sound along with my spoken instructions:

"Take a blue block and put it on top of a green block. Now take a red block and put it behind the blue block. Take a yellow block and put it on top of the green block." You can see this teaches or assumes other skills and knowledge as well, but the important thing was for Matt to focus on what I was saying, in spite of the interference of other sounds or voices.

The instructions and the background noises had to increase in complexity beyond what I could record myself, and that's when Judy Ball lent me tapes, not readily available in the marketplace at that time, so that I could continue Matt's training at home. Everyone's a caregiver.

The reason I tell this story, though, is that it's about patience. Repetition takes a lot of patience on the part of the repeater, especially if the repeater is a caregiver and human. In the case of a person with Alzheimer's or any kind of dementia, he will ask the same question time and time again, forgetting the answer. If the answer is recorded, the voice remains calm and quiet and is never irritated, like the voice on a tape recorder or, these days, like a robot.

Robots have now been developed and made available, at considerable expense, as caregivers. I'm sure the price will come down as the need becomes more common. I found a list on the net of the services a robot caregiver can provide, all useful, and some essential, to the well-being of an elderly person. Among other services they can:

- help with heavy lifting. Better than neighbours and exempt from legal complications in case of injury;
- serve as a communication tool. "Call John." Like the command to go and wash the clothes, it's easier for the technologically impaired than personally coping with FaceTime or Skype;
- provide reminders. A paper memo, a bulletin board or a computer calendar can do this, but one has to remember to look at the list and to follow up. A programmed robot can nag (patiently!);
- help with monitoring.

Online medical checks are becoming more and more common and life saving for people with diabetes or heart problems or epilepsy. Matt is epileptic and wears a MedicAlert necklace so that people on the street[63] will know what's wrong if he should have a seizure—an infrequent occurrence; it's controlled with drugs. Once, when he was between apartment mates, who must be assigned by Community Living, I requested an electronic monitor for him to wear when he was home alone. It was connected with his phone line so that help was available if he got into trouble.

Long before that, before my mother moved to Toronto, I hired a service to keep in touch with her daily. I don't know if this still exists as things get more and more technical, but it was designed to help two people per case. An older woman was paid to phone my mother once a day to chat and see how things were going. It didn't last long because Mom figured out that someone was being paid to do this, and she would have none of it. She feared being an expense or a burden.

---

[63] We depend on the kindness of strangers.

I fear it myself, ever since I gave up my car. As I reported in my introduction, I quit driving voluntarily as an ecological statement. I promised myself then that I would not be a burden to my mobile friends, begging lifts and help with errands. I bought a shopping cart for light, perishable or urgent items, and I have groceries delivered from my online orders. So far I have not resorted to home delivery of liquor.[64] But a friend warned me that I used the word "burden" too much. With robots there is never a burden. On we go!

Not even the most devoted family can do everything. Actually, no one can, but that's not the point that I have been discovering as I grow older and older. People are busy, and have their own difficulties to cope with and their own lives to live. I used to note when I was first widowed that the time I most missed other people was when others were most busy with their own concerns. I'm not sure robots can help with that. This is not about being a burden; this is about loneliness. I just have to get used to it.

Remember the movie *Cast Away*? (2000). Tom Hanks played a FedEx employee stranded on a desert island with one of his deliveries, a Wilson brand volleyball that became his companion. He called it Wilson and talked to it to stave off his loneliness and to keep from going squirrelly. I talk to myself all the time. I'm sure I wouldn't have any trouble talking to a robot.

There are ways of dealing with loneliness. It's not a problem exclusive to the aged. We all need caregivers; that is, people who care.

Caring for myself is an act of survival.

Audre Lorde (1934–1992)

---

[64] I have now, since I broke my wrist. Bottles are heavy.

CHAPTER ELEVEN

TAKING COMFORT

**There is nothing like staying
at home for real comfort.**

Jane Austen (1775–1817)

The very notion of comfort, let alone the actual state of being comfortable, is a fairly new one. The Canadian-American writer-architect Witold Rybczynski (b. 1943) scarcely encountered the concept of comfort during his first studies. His initial surprise was that it was *not* discussed. Nominated for the Governor General's Award for non-fiction, his book *Home: A Short History of an Idea* (1986) examines, among other things, the idea of comfort. He says that the word didn't appear in any of his courses, except once in reference to heating: the "comfort zone" for people was ideally about 70 degrees Fahrenheit. As we know, there's a lot more to comfort than that, although I must say, I do like to be warm.

Oddly enough, at least oddly to people who are still fooled by the cold implication in the name, Iceland is the warmest place in Europe. At least, it has been for me. Warmth is cheaper there because of the geothermal "built-in" heating provided by underground aquifers containing water up to 700 degrees

Fahrenheit and carried by pipelines to the cities. Houses are warm— there's no stingy electric heater in a room with a closed door to keep the heat in; no electric blanket to warm the bed but not the room, oh, but no fireplaces, I'm sorry to say, because wood is scarce.[65] But the streets are heated, the water is hot, the rooms are warm, and like other civilized places it has duvets. Happiness, and comfort, is a warm duvet.

I read a book about comfort because I wanted to know more. It wasn't much help. My memory of it is that it was by another architect who concentrated on porches and patios. I love them myself. My apartment balcony is my summer home. I guess you could call it a porch. I call it my cottage, but you could also call it my hermitage or ashram. It's my place of retreat but not my only source of comfort.

I looked up "creature comforts." As you might expect, there are heating firms whose ads offer creature comforts. And there are any number of pet stores named Creature Comforts (cute!) because they cater to all creatures, great and small. So do hotels and spas and travel agencies with human clients. Just what do creature comforts promise, and how does that relate to the aging traveller?

Comfort is, first of all, physical. The basic amenities of comfort are accepted to be food and warmth and sleeping facilities. I would add security to that list: safe accommodation would be good, and that would automatically ensure intangible but necessary peace of mind, certainly these days a great source of mental comfort. So am I saying don't make me nervous? Hardly. Isabella Bird or Freya Stark or Dervla Murphy[66] would scoff. So, for that matter, would Paul Theroux. He often seems crotchety to me, but he doesn't go

---

[65] A Drowning Pool where witches were immersed is one of the sights to see. Wood could not be spared to burn people.

[66] The Irish cycling tourist and travel writer once went 30 days without changing her clothes, probably not very comfortable.

looking for luxury or even comfort; in fact, he seems to avoid it. Maybe that's why he comes across as crotchety. Anyway, I have no desire to be intrepid, daunted, or uncomfortable. Maybe those hardy travellers don't need creature comforts, but I do.

Everyone needs food, not necessarily exotic. Michael Pollan (b. 1955) has written a number of award-winning books about food, but he is best and easily remembered for his rules for eating, summed up in three terse commands:

- ✓ Eat food
- ✓ Not too much
- ✓ Mostly plants

And I love his warning not to eat anything your great (great) grandmother wouldn't have recognized as food. All that processed stuff and refined sugar is what he means. Well, I'm a great-grandmother now, and I just want to say that I'm grateful for some food that I wasn't even aware of as a child, or even as a young housewife in Winnipeg, wishing for a new vegetable in the dead of winter. I have often said since then, "Where was zucchini when I needed it?" Or edamame, or fennel, or even snow pea pods. No doubt about it, the vegetables available in the northern hemisphere are not what they used to be, I'm happy to say.[67]

Aging travellers with guilt-free appetites will find safe, clean, good and recognizable food in most of the places they go. We are warned about salads and raw fruits in most places where the water is questionable. Just as the ice may not be safe in a glass of Perrier because its source is local water, so the raw vegetables are not safe if they've been washed in that same water. I found this out the hard way. Trusting a high-class travel agency during a trip to Kenya, I blithely ate everything, including the salads. Guess

---

[67]   Watch out for the locavore movement. If we who live in a cold climate stuck to it in winter, we'd all end up with scurvy.

what? I picked up a parasite that waited until I was on my way home from Nairobi to reveal itself. The trip arrangements had allowed me a layover in London for no extra fee, and I stopped for four days to see some theatre. I barely made it into the hotel room. I phoned room service for help: a bucket, more towels, extra blankets, tea, ice water, hard candies, everything I could think of to comfort me and treat my, as yet undiagnosed, ailment. Plugged up with Imodium, I did get to the theatre, although I spent one act of *Amadeus* in the ladies' room. I got a single scalped ticket to the new hot show *Cats*, and stayed in my seat in a miasma for which I was too embarrassed to apologize to my neighbours.

When I returned to Canada, I reported to the Tropical Disease Unit at Toronto General. My parasite was found and identified with a name that sounded like an Italian opera diva. I was told to avoid all dairy products for about 4 months, especially yogurt, as it provides a culture for growth. Take note.

I was going to Banff to work in the Advanced Writing Studio within that time frame. By the time I arrived at the residence, Lloyd Hall, with my papers and my luggage, I was parched and headed for the nearest water fountain. When I had finished quenching my thirst, I raised my head and read the sign warning people not to drink the water because it was contaminated with giardiasis, commonly known as "beaver fever." Oh, well, I'd just let the two of them fight it out. After 4 months, my Italian opera star took out her citizenship papers and left me, and I was okay with the beavers. After all, they were Canadian, though not, sadly, safe. So now we buy bottled water and pollute the Earth with plastic. I guess we should add clean water to the list of creature comforts.

I'll tell you one comfort that every traveller and every smart person over a certain age prizes above all else: naps. Daytime naps. Sleep is on the list of comforts, but naps are not specified. Naps are considered okay for children and the very elderly but not for real, grown-up (old) people. Nonsense. Scientists have been conducting sleep surveys and collecting nap reports. Naps are more complicated than you might think and more beneficial, not only for old folks. There are several kinds of naps:

1. **Power naps** are familiar in this age of big business and credited with increasing productivity, for executives only.
2. **Catnap** is an old-fashioned term, fallen out of favour, but delicious, the kind favoured by old ladies like me.
3. **Caffeine naps** are new to me. Apparently if you hit the pillow immediately after a cup of coffee, before the effects of the caffeine kick in, about 15 minutes, you can have a great nap.
4. **Polyphasic sleeping**, or regularly spaced short naps, is a term familiar to shift-workers, emergency care workers, military personnel, medical interns and so on: people who are compelled by their jobs to work 24 hours and more at a stretch and who, therefore, must catch some sleep before they crash. So far, even with scheduled naps, deficits in alertness and performance are noticeable, remedied only by proper sleep.

A condition called "sleep inertia" can occur; you know that feeling when you wake up from a short nap and you don't feel like getting up because you're still half asleep? The nice thing about being old is that you don't have to. It's one of the perks of being retired or semi- or self-employed. But watch out for your employer; she can be a stickler, and you have to be careful with your excuses because she knows when your grandmother died.

I do not take sleeping pills. I've been given two in my life: one on the night my husband died, and the second on the night I came home from hospital after having had 5/8ths of my stomach removed. I think the whole idea of eight hours of sleep as a requirement of good health dates only from the Industrial Revolution, when more people were working on a regular, usually

9-to-5, schedule, and a regular sleeping pattern was considered (by the employers) necessary for maximum efficiency.

"Segmented sleep" was an accepted norm in earlier times, in medieval England and France and elsewhere, with many literary references (Chaucer, for example) confirming it was an accepted pattern. "First sleep" was followed by a wakeful but peaceful time, good for contemplation or sex, then followed by "second sleep" in the early morning hours; in other words, a natural polyphasic sleep pattern.

Dr. Sara C. Mednick, assistant professor at the Department of Psychology at the University of California, Riverside, is the author of *Take a Nap! Change Your Life* (2006). She has been studying sleep in a variety of pursuits, such as "creative problem solving, verbal memory, perceptual learning, object learning, and statistical learning." She says her research shows that "napping maintains and even boosts our skills." You probably already knew that, but it's nice to be reassured. Among other things, naps keep you looking younger and build up your stamina. These are useful benefits for an aging traveller to enjoy. Chalk up napping as a required creature comfort.

Warmth is a top priority for me. One of my rules of travel (see Appendix) is always to take socks and a sweater because you might be cold in bed. In my travelling days, when I was doing workshops or readings in schools, libraries or community clubs, I was often billeted in a private home, and I was often cold without an extra blanket. A couple of times I resorted to taking a rug from the floor. I put it on top of my other covers to be warm. That's when I devised the rule about always taking socks and a sweater. Mind you, hotels can be difficult, too. Modern hotels are hermetically sealed; windows cannot be opened. I find it difficult to turn off air conditioning. At least there are extra blankets in the cupboard. We're warned now about mites in the bedspread. I'm too old to worry about mites. There are too many other things to fuss about. I need that bedspread.

Perhaps Alvin Toffler (1928–2016) made one's misgivings easier to deal with. I think of his book *Future Shock* when I travel, perhaps not in the way that he intended. Simplified, his message, as I understood it, was: with too many changes in too little time, beware of information overload. So do what you can to keep things familiar. I apply his advice when I travel. It began when I was travelling a lot with a new book each year when even modest, obscure writers like me were treated to a book tour to publicize one's effort. These tours were not travel as such; they were a kind of obstacle course. The if-this-is-Edmonton-it-must-be-Tuesday schedule reduces Canada to a series of plane rides and television studios and presents a challenge to someone who has a horror of repeating herself. You'd think with an attitude like that, I would welcome daily change, but not when it's too rapid and inexorable. As Emerson said, roughly, wherever you go you take you with you, and in a situation like this, that is, cross-Canada on speed, you're lucky if you do.[68]

So I was grateful to Toffler for his suggestions on how to cope with frequent travel. I *think* I adapted my routine from his suggestions. Briefly, I take my familiar habits with me as much as I can. Of course, I can't get up and swim everywhere, unless I'm in a hotel, but I can have tea in bed and write and sort out the tramlines to be dealt with each day. The idea is to establish your base, deal with the familiar, and then you're set to absorb, assimilate and proceed with the new. So there you are, here we are, comfortable and secure and familiar. Travel is so broadening!

We all function better with a familiar regimen. My youngest son, as you know by now, is challenged and epileptic; he must have a familiar, regular routine. He was 6 in 1967, when the whole country was tipping into the Atlantic Ocean as Canadians headed to Montreal for Expo '67. With our four children, we headed out from our home in Winnipeg, intent on celebrating Canada's

---

[68]   I think I left me behind in Grande Prairie once.

Centennial. This was their first big car trip. As the first day was drawing to a close, Matt started to worry.

"Going home soon?" he asked. "Dinner soon? Bed soon?"

No, I explained. We were going to find a motel, and we would have a swim and dinner and go to bed for the night. And that's what we did. He accepted that.

The next day we drove on and as the day was coming to an end, he asked:

"Swim soon? Dinner soon? Bed soon?"

He had adapted to the new ritual. Old people need ritual, too, and they can adapt. We all can. Even the Merry Prankster Ken Kesey (1935–2001) said, "Ritual is necessary for us to know anything."

According to my online dictionary, "ritual" is "a series of actions or type of behavior regularly and invariably followed." "Routine" is "a sequence of actions regularly followed; a fixed program." Not quite the same thing, at least, not to my mind. Ritual to me has a magical property and yet is more formal; routine is more tedious. Perhaps ritual is more reassuring because there's something mystic about it, but in the end, routine has much the same effect. They are both comforting. They give shape to our days and to what's going on. We need them both.

I do love the idea of ritual.

Sarah Silverman (b.1970)

CHAPTER TWELVE

CHOOSING

Two roads diverged in a wood, and I,
I took the one less travelled by,
And that has made all the difference.

Robert Frost (1874–1963)

When my children were very little, I followed the advice of some child psychologists and tried to give them a feeling of control in their small, regulated world.

"What colour socks would you like, red or blue?"

"Do you want apple juice or orange juice?"

"Shall we go to the park or the zoo?"

They often took a while to make the choices, obviously weighing the possibilities very carefully and savouring their control. I read just recently that the same courtesy is being extended to people in some retirement homes, senior citizens' residences and other euphemistically named but necessary living arrangements, with menu selection and movie choices, allowing them a bland, comforting simulacrum of independence.

Some of us may be grown-up, or not quite old, but we are no different. We like to pretend we have some control over our lives.

We have very little choice in what happens to us. Stuff happens, and we can seldom do anything to avoid it. Sometimes we can choose what to do about it, or we can choose how we feel about it.

My husband died suddenly a long time ago now. Obviously, I couldn't do anything about that. I had to go on living, reluctantly at first. He was survived, as the obituary reported, by four children, who needed me to help them grow up, so I hung in there.

First, as I officially launched my career as a writer—I had always written—but as I started to be a *professional* writer, trying to make enough money for us to live on, and then, as the money actually started to trickle in and people wanted to see/hear what I had to say, I began to travel. First it was for business, and then for pleasure as well as business—one of the perks of freelance writing. I became interested in what I was doing, not only for the income but also for the experiences.

Bill Wylie was the most interesting person I have ever known, smart and funny and kind and thoughtful—I try not to put him on a pedestal. I never knew what he was going to say next. After a day apart, he would come in the door and break me up with a single comment. Well, so, I said to myself after he was gone, "Life had better be interesting or I'm having none of it." Really. It's a corollary of my rule to have a reason to get out of bed in the morning, and it's a choice one makes.

Second, a few years later I took Matt to Scotland to meet his father's side of the family. His siblings had already done that, being interested in their roots, and I thought Matt and I ought to meet these dear people as well. As the plane was taking off, I did my usual spot check, summing up my life and assessing how everyone would get along without me. As the children grew older, I had ticked off each one of them as capable of going on alone, except Matt. He had taken more time, still does. Of course, one never stops being a mother, but you can't pause and totally relax as readily with a challenged child, no matter how old he is. Anyway, he was with me, so there was nothing to worry about. I told him that.

"We're together, Matt, so it doesn't matter if we crash."

He was sitting there with the headphones on, smiling, nodding his head as he listened to music, sipping a soda and having a good time. He took off the headphones to hear me, and I repeated what I had said.

"It's okay if we crash," I said.

"Come on!!" It was a protest. He was not one bit willing to die. He was choosing life.

The glass is half full or half empty, a cliché supposed to indicate whether the viewer is a pessimist or an optimist. Sure, it's in the eye of the beholder. It's a choice.

Oscar Wilde said, "there are moments when one has to choose between living one's own life, fully, entirely, completely—or dragging out some false, shallow, degrading existence ... Choose!"

It's a journey, and I seem always to have chosen Frost's less-travelled road. So many moments, so many roads, so many choices, and somehow they all add up to where I am right now at this moment. This moment in my life has taken a long time to arrive. Sometimes, at milestone events, I look back and think of how much I have lost and changed and moved on. I'm not feeling sorry for myself; I'm just making a list. I left my hometown and early friends, thereby losing much of my familiar identity.[69] I have left behind homes and furniture and belongings, more and more, many times. I left my marriage, perforce—or, rather, my marriage left me— and another identity dissolved, although I remained married to the middle class for quite a while, which, like my marriage, ended up leaving me. And then other people started leaving, not through distance but through death.

---

[69] Actually, I've written a book about it: *Life's Losses: Living Through Grief, Bereavement and Sudden Change*, Macmillan Canada, 1996.

The old woman in my play *A Place on Earth* comments, "It's getting so I know more people in the cemetery than I do on the street." My current line is that I feel like a duck in a shooting gallery with all the targets being picked off around me. So what or who is left? Well, as the Sondheim song goes, "I'm still here."

And everyone, everything around me has a history, with me by accident or by choice? Take furniture, for instance. I did, for a while, but I kept dropping off my possessions as I moved on, just like those settlers on their journey west, leaving behind the burden of their belongings as they travelled.

Perhaps a history of such losses would fit better within the chapter about downsizing, but downsizing implies more conscious choices, not sudden imperative decisions thrust upon one. Most of my possessions seem now to have come to me or remained with me by happenstance. Well, that's okay, too. I mustn't forget that I'm on a trip, and I don't want to carry too much baggage. Remember the Bruce Trail!

Speaking of which, I am still travelling, and I am still getting ready to go somewhere. Travelling lighter is only part of it. I am consciously remembering my past, how history, both personal and public, has influenced my choices. By analyzing my past, perhaps I can learn about my ultimate destination—at least the penultimate one. Be prepared, they say, and I hope I am. Not everyone is.

I remember when I went on that safari in East Africa, one of our fellow travellers insisted on being left behind at a posh resort while the rest of the group went on to stay in tents and hunt wild animals with their cameras. The trip was hardly spartan. The tent arrangements were very comfortable, and we alternated between tent stops and resort breaks. But our travel mate said she didn't expect it to be so dusty and hot on the veldt and she didn't like her tent-mate. (You should have heard what her assigned partner thought of her.) See, she hadn't done her homework, and she made an uninformed choice in taking the trip in the first place.

We all take risks when we choose to travel, but let them be calculated risks, at least. When I was in Hawaii (not my choice: I was engaged to speak at a Million Dollar Round Table conference), my hosts left me to my own devices, so I had to fill in time until I was due to perform. Rather than sit alone beside a pool, I chose a bunch of touristy activities, like a luau; a tour of the Arizona (the aircraft carrier that is a tomb and a memorial for all the Americans who died on board during the attack on Pearl Harbor); and a flight in a small plane over the active volcanoes. Of course, I was nervous.

So I wrote a note and left it on the dresser in my hotel room. It read, "To Whom It May Concern: if anything happens to me, please do not ship my body back to Canada. Just bury me here." Signed, etc. Since then, I've taken out trip insurance. That hadn't occurred to me. And there are rules about being planted where you fall. You might not be welcome.

I've always had this vision, conceived of seeing too many historical sea voyages on TV, of a body being draped in a flag and dropped into the sea. I actually wondered whether I should carry a Canadian flag with me on a long cruise so as to be prepared. However, I discovered that there is a clause in the travel insurance document, allowing X amount of money for the "repatriation of remains". Apparently, you *can* go home again, in fact, it's required. Still …

I have a friend whose husband suffered a fatal heart attack while they were on holiday in Cuba. Red tape and awkward, time-consuming, expensive arrangements exacerbated her grief and pain. Until she got the body back, there was no closure, either. So this is something else you have to take into account as you travel into old age. Not just how much money do you have, but how far do you want to go? How much do you lust for adventure? Creature comforts and safety become more and more important.

I have made choices while actually on a trip, when I realized that enough was enough. In Machu Picchu I did *not* take the three-day hike up to the site; I took the Toonerville Trolley instead, and it was fun. I merely walked the Sun Trail one morning. That afternoon, I had a nap and did *not* climb the other mountain in the rain. In Ireland, I did *not* leave my ship to take a rough boat ride to the Giant's Causeway. I stayed back on board and had a wonderful conversation with a woman who was dying of cancer and who had a smile like a rainbow for the remission she had been granted. Talking to her was a learning experience. I like to think I am getting smart in my old age. I still have a few things on my bucket list that I'm going to attempt while I still can. Or not. We'll see.

It's all a matter of choice. Choices may be simple and non-threatening, like selecting one's dinner from a restaurant menu, or more significant and lasting, like deciding on a study course or a career offer or a life-mate. They can also be dangerous. The American critic and journalist Alexander Woollcott (1887–1943) once said, "All the things I really like to do are either illegal, immoral, or fattening." Today, they're worse: they are addictive, lethal, or fatal. Be careful what you choose.

That's the key advice in a series of inspirational messages I came across on the Internet, with a list of wishes (for strength, assistance, courage, etc.) and the oblique way in which these desires are answered. I understand that. One request I made in my life revealed such an obliquity. I asked for patience, and I got Matthew. My challenged son required a lot of patience, still does. I don't always deliver, but I'm better than I used to be. If I were to ask and choose again, I'd ask for the same thing and be grateful. I'm thankful for Matt. I won't go into detail because I've written a lot about him elsewhere.[70] He became my Muse. You get the hand

---

[70]   *The Book of Matthew,* a biography; *Boy in a Cage,* a chamber opera; *Jason,* a one-hander play/monologue; *Six Lost Hours,* a movie. All have been produced and/or published except the film, for which I still have hope.

you're dealt, but you can still choose how to play it. I wonder what Matt would choose.

I know my father said you're only sorry for what you didn't do, and so did Mark Twain (or not). There's always compensation in some form or other. You just have to recognize it. Count your blessings. My father used to do that on every trip he ever took. When I was still a teenager and travelling with my parents, mostly by car in North America, "We drove 400 miles today," he'd say, "and we crossed 2 states." He'd go on from there to notable events, even if there weren't any particularly notable, and I'd say, "Yes, yes, that's how it was."

He did that when he was dying, too, giving me the opportunity to assess his life and to say goodbye. "I've had 65 good years (he died on his 66th birthday), and I've had a good life, a good wife and 2 wonderful children. I served in 2 wars and survived both of them."

And I'd say, "Yes, yes, that's how it was."

That was part of getting ready. He was choosing to go and preparing me to stay.

Be careful what you pray for. You just might get it.

Larry Dossey (b.1940)

CHAPTER THIRTEEN

GOING SOLO

The whole point of travelling is to arrive alone.

Paul Theroux (b. 1941)

What's true of travel is also true of life: you must be prepared to be alone. "Old age," as so many people have said that I don't know to whom to attribute it, although I first heard it from an aunt of mine who suffered from emphysema, "is not for sissies." Neither is travel.

You've heard it before: Alone but not lonely. It sounds like a glass-half-full cliché to cheer you up or knock you down, depending on which direction you are looking: up or down. Solitude is the good side of loneliness. You have to be careful, though. It can be soul-destroying, especially, I have read, in prisons in the United States. Solitary confinement has been proven to be mentally damaging and is now acknowledged as a severe form of torture.

Some creative people welcome prolonged periods of (self-imposed) solitude as an aid to artistic expression. I do. I like it. I'm not an artist, just a run-of-the-mill writer, but it helps me to focus.

The English psychiatrist and author Anthony Storr (1920–2001) published his book *Solitude: A Return to the Self* in 1988, and it has become a classic. The subtitle says it all. Not a bad thing. Storr's good news is that you don't have to be a genius or a great artist to profit from solitude; it appeals to and benefits average folks, too. And it is the self with which we are concerned on this journey, dragging it along doggedly as we go the distance.

Most life travellers are aware of the hazards. Most life travellers are alone. We know that 75 percent of women are alone by the time they're 65. On the other hand, most men who survive to that age and past—and their life expectancy is greater now— still have women to take care of them (part of the remaining 25 percent, I guess). No more stats. By the time you reach my age, as I've pointed out, fewer and fewer of my contemporaries are busy with living husbands. Advice columns for the aging are about companionship, or the lack of, and the advice is to cultivate younger friends, the inference being that they won't die on you. It's inevitable. My current friends now are all at least 10 to 12 years younger than I am, if you consider that young. I don't. When I was Canada's professional widow, travelling around the country with my hard-won advice, I used to say that it might be a good idea for a woman to marry a man 5 to 10 years younger so that she might be guaranteed a companion in her later years. Until the day one woman put up her hand and told me that she used to think so, too, and did just that, married a younger man, but he had a stroke and didn't die, so she was going to the hospital every day to visit him, though he didn't know who she was. So much for that theory. No guarantees, ever.

Peggy Woodgreen, the old woman in my play *A Place on Earth,* speculates about that. She says that a woman should marry a man at least 10 years younger so he won't die on her. But that would mean, she goes on, that a woman of 20 would marry a boy of 10. She pauses, thinking about that, and wonders: "What would they talk about?"

This word "companion" keeps coming up. Is companionship the antidote to solitude? This is from the online version of the *Oxford Dictionary of English;*

- traveling companion | figurative: fear became my constant companion.
- a person who shares the experiences of another, esp. when these are unpleasant or unwelcome: my companions in misfortune.
- a person's long-term sexual partner outside marriage.
- a person, esp. an unmarried or widowed woman, employed to live with and assist another.

Oh, dear. My first thought when I read that was of a dear friend whose most constant, beloved companion, his dog, died. He went berserk. His dog was all he had, and he suffered all the horrendous withdrawal symptoms one suffers upon the death of a loved one, whether animal or human. No one has a corner on pain. I wouldn't wish that kind of grief on anyone, though most of us are condemned to experience it sooner or later. All I could offer my friend was the weak reassurance that I drew from what I called "beads of respite."

I found, in the first terrible time after Bill died, that if I could find one tolerable moment in the day—perhaps walking with one of my children or having coffee with a friend—if I could hold that brief time like a bead of time in my fingers, it helped. Gradually, and very slowly, I strung together a few beads until at last I had a short, fragile necklace, free of pain.

Am I still discussing companionship? I guess I am. I quit smoking years ago, one of the hardest things I ever did. I would never start again because quitting was too hard. I remember taking up a pipe as one of my first ineffective attempts. This was years before Nicorette or any of the surrogates available today. I bought a cute little pipe with a rhinestone-studded bowl and puffed away at it at parties where I used to smoke a lot. I found that after a pipe, there was nothing I wanted as much as a cigarette, the Real Thing. (My apologies to dedicated pipe smokers.) To me, pipe smoking was like masturbation, not nearly as good as the real thing.

So how's that for an introduction to sex? A companion, as noted above, can be a sexual partner. So what do you do without one? Here is where I must part with my younger readers. I had to deal with sex in a few of my other books, when I was younger,- with sex and physical need and love. I used to pray for the sap to stop running so I wouldn't be so needy. It finally has stopped, I'm not exactly happy to say, but I'm relieved. If I had a partner, a live-in companion, it would be different, but I don't. And I never did take to a pipe.

I don't cry any more, either, not that I don't feel strong emotions. I do. But my heart has been gouged so deeply to dry bedrock that I don't cry.[71] I also am aware that compared to some, to most human beings in the world today, I have suffered nothing. As I say, I don't claim a corner on pain, and I don't deserve to cry. Tears are healthy, it is said, providing an escape valve. Self-pity is not. So I'm alone. So what?

Surveys—always the surveys!—reveal that loneliness breaks hearts, literally. Loneliness is bad for your health. Unwanted, neglected people feel singled out (pun intended) and don't feel loved or healthy. Lonely people have higher blood pressure than non-lonely people and that increases the risk of heart attack or stroke. Involuntary solitude is damaging, we've already established that. Self-imposed isolation is not so bad. That brings us back to choice. You may not have chosen to be alone, but you can still choose how you feel about it, and what you're going to do about

---

[71] Beware of sweeping statements. I have just learned that one of my few remaining contemporaries has gone into palliative care, with three months to live. I cried.

it. You don't need me to tell you that, so I won't. This is a memoir, not a self-help book.[72]

Scottish novelist Andrew O'Hagan (b.1968) recommends travelling alone. In an article in the *New York Times Style Magazine* he acknowledges the idea that you should always travel with someone you love, which is why he goes alone. Like most other self-indulgent, thoughtful travellers, however, he reports that you meet yourself. I suppose how you feel about that depends on how you feel about yourself.

That brings us perilously close to Aristotle and his idea of the union of body and soul that comprises the self.

Hylomorphism, anyone?[73] Too much.

Say not, 'I have found the path of the soul.'
Say rather, 'I have met the soul walking upon my path.'

Kahlil Gibran (1883–1931)

---

[72] Hard to believe, isn't it?

[73] Hylomorphism is a philosophical theory developed by Aristotle, which conceives being as a compound of matter and form. *Wikipedia*.

CHAPTER FOURTEEN

FINDING SELF

**Now I become myself. It's taken
Time, many years and places**

May Sarton (1912–1995)

I guess I qualify to be myself. I've put in the time: it's taken many years and a lot of places. It's not that simple a formula, though.

Geriatricians[74] are telling people how to take care of themselves, as if they were offering a foolproof magic elixir. The advice is not exclusive to the elderly and certainly no secret. We all know the drill: good nutrition but less food, lots of sleep, less medicine, lots of exercise, less stress, oh, and how about more laughter? My father the doctor used to say there was more good medicine delivered by Wayne and Shuster[75] than by William Osler.[76] You know the saying "laughter is the best medicine." Believe it.

---

[74] With a population of 32 million, Canada has 500 geriatricians, not all of them in private practice. Compare this to Sweden with 9 million people, served by 500 geriatricians.

[75] Johnny Wayne (1918–1990) and Frank Shuster (1916–2002) were a Canadian comedy team, well known in the U.S. because they appeared on The Ed Sullivan Show 67 times.

[76] Called "the Father of Modern Medicine," Sir William Osler (1849–1919) was an influential Canadian doctor and, incidentally, a practical joker.

Norman Cousins (1915–1990) was a great advocate of laughter. The American writer and peace activist was a favourite of mine when he was editor of the *Saturday Review,* to which I subscribed when I had neither the time nor the money to afford much intellectual input.[77] Cousins trained himself to laugh in order to survive a serious disease. His book *Anatomy of an Illness* (1979) describes his self-treatment: masses of vitamin C and daily doses of Marx Brothers films. He writes, "I made the joyous discovery that ten minutes of genuine belly laughter had an anesthetic effect and would give me at least two hours of pain-free sleep."

Laughter is a choice we make, and it's about the best there is. Do not take it lightly. Most people do, especially literary critics. They think if a work is funny, it can't be important. Wrong. I'm dealing with serious issues, about the most serious there are: life and death and in between, the in-between being the state of mind you bring to bear on them. That's you, the awareness, the consciousness, aha—the self! That's me, anyway. I'm skating on the edge of an abyss, and I know it. I'm dealing with concepts that great minds have struggled with over the centuries. Not surprisingly, they don't agree.

Emerson (1803–1882), you may remember, said that no matter how far you go, you take you with you, the implication being that you are inescapable and unchanging. On the other hand, the French writer Georges Sand (1804–1876), considering herself more aged than we would today, wrote in her diary in 1869:

> —and now I am very old, gently traversing my sixty-fifth year … My plan in jotting down these thoughts and feelings was based on a theory I once believed in. I used to imagine that I could

---

[77] I first read Susan Sontag's essay "The Double Standard of Aging" (1979) in that magazine.

pick up my own identity from time to time and carry it on. Can one thus resume one's self? Can one know one's self? Is one ever *somebody*? I don't know anything about it any more. It now seems to me that one changes from day to day and that every few years one becomes a new being.

A new being.

Whereas Doris Lessing (1919–2013) comments on the fact that you never change, you're always here: "The great secret that all old people share is that you really haven't changed in seventy or eighty years. Your body changes, but you don't change at all. And that, of course, causes great confusion." I think maybe she means the confusion experienced by others who want to treat her differently.

All writers seem to know the entity they're dealing with when they write about themselves, and they take it for granted that we know, too, about our selves. But *self* as we conceive of it today did not exist until the invention of the printing press. Gutenberg, thou shouldst be with us at this hour!

When I was working on my book about women's diaries,[78] I had to find out how and when women in history first learned to read and write.[79] I worked my way up to the printing press and the wider dissemination of reading material. After that, it was easy. Initially, I made discoveries I hadn't expected to find about the origins of self.

At first, books were very rare, as rare as the people who could read them. There were designated readers who replaced the

---

[78]   *Reading Between the Lines: The Diaries of Women.* Key Porter Books, 1995.

[79]   The literate ones have been rare throughout history. Of the world's illiterate today, 80 percent of them are women.

wandering minstrels and storytellers and who read one book to a group of listeners. When a book finally fell into the hands of a reader and he had it all to himself, he read it aloud so he could listen because that's what he was accustomed to. You still see people who mouth the words to themselves as they read. Gradually, the words and thoughts began to enter the reader's mind silently, and they became private, for his own interpretation and for his use only. This processing produced distinctive thoughts belonging solely to the reader, and he recognized his thoughts as his very own, and his private processor as Self. This is oversimplified, of course. Before "self" emerged as a noun, defined as the distinctive essence of an individual, it was only an adjective, separated by a hyphen from words that identified its function: self-centered, self-control, self-conscious, self-confident, self-destructive, self-hatred, self-image. The list goes on, but I'll stop at one that has its own weaknesses and critics: self-help. The point is that without the qualifier, "self" became synonymous with soul, soul with life force, life force with spirit, spirit with identity, identity with ego, and one definition of ego is "part of mind containing consciousness." One thing leads to another: self, soul, mind, consciousness, and awareness. (Once you have found it, never let it go.) Until death shall you part. End of the journey? As far as we know.

This is one of the great perks of age—that is, if one retains some health and some competence *to keep going along the path*. Keep on keeping on and keep on surviving. I am grateful for it, for survival. I went through many of the usual traumata of life, often at an earlier age than most of my contemporaries: difficulties with a challenged child, premature widowhood, major surgery, and financial crises—the latter never stop. But each time I "front fate abreast,"[80] I emerge not only stronger but also more confident. I always quote that line from *Deor's Lament*, the Old English

---

[80] Lovely phrase, written by Emily Murphy (1868–1933), aka Janey Canuck, Canadian writer and early feminist.

poem about the lone survivor of terrible hardships: "That passed, so may this."

According to yet another survey, this equanimity is common among older people, among survivors. One of the most interesting perks of living so long is that I know the endings of most stories. It gives me a feeling of continuity, of being centred in my own story.

1. What happened to the married woman who left her husband and children and ran off with her young fencing master?
2. How did the child turn out who was the daughter of two lesbian mothers and a turkey baster?
3. Did the divorced son-in-law who split for Mexico with his son get away with it?
4. How long did my friends' face-lifts last?
5. What did the woman do after her husband absconded to the Cayman Islands with all the cash, leaving her broke at the beginning of winter with no money to pay the heating bills?

Well, here's how they ended:

1. Everyone predicted dire results and a sad, lonely ending, but she lived happily ever after, and last I heard, her young man had stayed with her and looked after her in her old age.
2. The little girl ended up so straight that she drove her two parents crazy with her fussing about clothes and make-up and boys.
3. The little boy missed his mother so much that the father gave in and took his son home. No charges were laid.
4. Not long enough.
5. She got a good lawyer and remarried and stayed warm.

If the short-term memory starts to fade, the long-term memory delivers bright, sharply etched images, as well as the history and dénouement of the events, and if I forget some of the details, who's going to correct me? "The past is a foreign country; they do things differently there."[81] That's a famous line, relatively recent, oft repeated (by me), but with the resonance of a proverb.

I think age is the last great frontier. We keep pushing the boundaries back, and that's good, but we keep trying to play young, to extend the limits of an earlier stage without attaining the final stage of growth—as defined by the psychologist and psychoanalyst Erik Erikson (1902–1994).

Erikson defined eight stages of development or growth:

- basic trust
- autonomy
- purpose/initiative
- competence
- fidelity/identity
- intimacy
- generativity
- ego integrity

Not everyone reaches ego integrity, when, if one is wise enough, one can battle despair.

Those who may try to stop us or denigrate the wisdom that awaits deserve our rage, not our supplication. To be truly creative and fulfilled, we must live out the last third (fourth?) of our lives as if we've only just begun. Even the setbacks, obstacles and handicaps are part of the challenge. For those of us lucky enough to explore the outermost limits of age—and there are going to be more and more, in greater numbers, coming right along—a new experience awaits, and a new discovery of self.

---

[81] Opening line from *The Go-Between* by L.P. Hartley (1895–1972)

I'm looking forward to it.

**Loneliness is the poverty of self;
solitude is the richness of self.**

May Sarton (1912–1995)

CHAPTER FIFTEEN

DISCOVERING

**We can have in life but one great experience
at best, and the secret of life is to reproduce that
experience as often as possible.**

Oscar Wilde (1854–1900)

Epiphany has almost lost the power of its original meaning: "The manifestation of Christ to the Gentiles as represented by the Magi." Now the word is more commonly used and understood in its secular meaning (the third definition in my online dictionary): "a moment of sudden revelation or insight." It is often referred to as an "Aha! moment," or a "light bulb moment," or by an easy segue: "a Eureka moment."[82]

Mihaly Csikszentmihalyi (b. 1934) is a Hungarian-American psychologist best known for his theory of "Flow," a mental state of immersion or involvement with a satisfying activity. In his 1990 book *Flow: The Psychology of Optimal Experience*, he lists six factors necessary for the flow experience to take place. He says it helps if you have an "autotelic personality," which he describes as

---

[82]   I wish I had one now.

an individual "who can learn to enjoy situations that most other people would find miserable." Perhaps that describes people like traveller Freya Stark, for example, or Paul Theroux.

Almost 30 years earlier, the American psychologist Abraham Maslow (1908–1970) published *Toward a Psychology of Being* (first published 1962). He posited a list of five hierarchical needs as a pyramid, starting with the basic physiological essentials. Food and survival are at the bottom, rising through the demands for safety, love and belonging, and self-esteem, culminating in the highest need, which is for self-actualization, which not everyone can achieve, being too preoccupied with fulfilling the basic necessities. Perhaps only the autotelic personality can manage it.

Not to denigrate the work of these two men, but I saw them catch on with the pop psychologists. "Flow" and "peak experience" became buzzwords. I heard them. I heard a friend tell me who had attended a nice enough Mozart concert that he had enjoyed a peak experience. Wow. I see the same indiscriminate knee-jerk enthusiasm in the now habitual standing ovation in theatres. Hardly an epiphany.

Some wag has said that "epiphany" is a classy word for the realization that you've been practically retarded all these years.[83] Anyway, that's how these revelations strike you, if you're lucky, or maybe you're smarter than I am and they hit you right away, unlike my delayed insight about zebras. With me, it's more like a slow dawning.

I was ahead of myself in school, not advanced, not really advanced; people just kept thinking I was smarter than I was. I kept up, though not with everything. Because I was 2 years younger than my peers, I missed out on the scatological talk in the washrooms and the sex talk in the bushes. So I was 17 in third year university, taking double honours French and English, handling it all coolly, and I could speak knowledgeably about the

---

[83] I think I may have said it, but I'm not sure.

blood-stained cloth in Gide's *Les Faux Monnayeurs*, recognizing it as a symbol of a woman's lost virginity, hymen ruptured and all that, but I had no idea what I was talking about.

My brother ordered a book, delivered in discreet brown-paper wrapping, that he gave me to read. It was about SEX, the basics, and I was fascinated. The day after I read it, I was on my way out to the university on the bus and I saw a dog humping another dog and I said, almost out loud, "Is *that* what they're doing?" That was a Eureka, Aha! Epiphany.

As I say, slow.

It seems the older I get, the less I know. But I keep on making startling discoveries, and that's why I'm not quite ready to leave yet. I'm not old enough. I still have more to learn. The passing show keeps on being terribly interesting and often very funny. The self I thought I found yesterday has changed, a little fragmented today, ditzy even, but meandering right along. Or is it maundering?

I'm still exploring, still searching for epiphanies, my own or someone else's. Paul Theroux has produced a wonderful book, *The Tao of Travel: Enlightenments from Lives on the Road* (2011), with his own accounts, impressions, advice and comments along with excerpts from dozens of other travellers. At the end of the book, he offers his own epiphanies, the unexpected happening that he says "transforms the whole nature of the trip and stays with the traveller." I won't describe his epiphanies, but it is important to note Theroux's analysis of the "fundamental quest in travel." It is "the search for the unexpected. The discovery of an unanticipated pleasure can be life-changing."

Hindsight can make such a discovery seem so self-evident as not to be a revelation at all, simply a fact hitherto unacknowledged. Not so. Something has to happen to bring it home, to register in the conscious mind. That something, of course, is the Aha! moment, the light bulb that never flashed before but that now will never go out. Throughout my life, I have experienced at least three wondrous epiphanies that meet Theroux's requirements for being "life-changing."

ONE:

I was 16 in second year arts at the University of Manitoba when I met Bill Wylie. He was 20, in third year commerce. He had a crush on a sorority sister[84] of mine, and he would come looking for her in the library on my campus. She never went to the library. Failing her, he would ask me for coffee and a walk, and we became friends. I dated other boys; we never had any actual dates for almost 4 years. But one time, a later dating time, he came in for coffee after a movie and we talked. We always talked; we never stopped talking. I don't know what was so special about the talk that night but something he said touched me. He kissed me goodnight. I don't think he had ever kissed me before. Anyway, it was like Hemingway: "the earth moved," or something did. I pulled back and looked up at him (I always liked tall men).

"What are you doing?"

"Kissing you." Did he say it? I don't know.

"No, what are you *doing?*"

You see, that was an epiphany. Something inside me lit up, something moved over and made a space for him. Years later, after he died, I felt that space move outside me, and I compared it to the white space in a child's sticker book that was supposed to be filled in, but the stickum had gone.

TWO:

I actually had bleeding ulcers before Bill died. We know now that it isn't tension or stress that causes ulcers; it's a bacterium[85] that can be treated with a pill instead of a knife. We didn't know it then. So I had lost a lot of blood, and I was in the hospital for a blood transfusion. I was asleep and woke up to see Bill sitting there in the chair across from me, just sitting there and loving me.

---

[84]   We had sororities in Canada in those days.

[85]   Helicobacter pylori bacterium.

And that was an epiphany. He didn't have to say anything. I didn't need the word. I kept that image of him in my head for years. I can still conjure it up. It was more than life changing; it was life assuring, my shield and my touchstone.

THREE:

I had never thought of myself as pretty. I was fat and smart as a kid at school, and later, I had a fat self-image; fat, but flat chested at a time in history when the ideal female body had breasts like the nose cone of a B-52. I was still sort of smart, though. My line was that I was brought up smart, not pretty. I realized some time then that I could never lure a man across a crowded room, but if he got close enough to listen to me, I might attract him with my wit. Nothing Bill could say could convince me that I had any sex appeal, not to denigrate his taste, but he liked me before he loved me. I clung to that.

So a couple of years after he had died, when a man hit on me, I found it hard to believe. He couldn't possibly find me attractive, could he? I was puzzling about that the day after the encounter as I got into the car. And I heard Bill's voice, loud, as clear as if he were sitting beside me:

"Now do you believe me?"

Epiphany!

Well, that's personal, insights from my private life. Epiphanies are very private. But I had others, related to my creative life, useful, informative and astonishing. I wonder where epiphany ends and serendipity begins.

I've always loved the word serendipity and its provenance. Horace Walpole (1717–1797) coined it, from his affection for a fairy tale, in translation from the Persian,[86] *The Three Princes of Serendip*, in which the princes make fortunate discoveries, by accident and their own smarts, of things they weren't actually looking for but were happy to find. So the word means "the

---

[86]   Serendip is Persian or Urdu for Sri Lanka.

occurrence and development of events by chance in a happy or beneficial way,"(the online dictionary) or, being in the right place at the right time.

I was fortunate enough to have two serendipities happen to me with regard to my writing pursuits. The first was when I was in Boston/Cambridge on a Mary Bunting Fellowship at Radcliffe/ Harvard, working on a play about Alice James (1848–1892), sister of the novelist Henry James and the psychologist/philosopher William James. I was living in Boston with my daughter and her family and working in an office in Cambridge, provided by the Mary Bunting Institute. It so happened that I had finished my research to the point where I was ready to write my first draft, just as the American Thanksgiving was approaching. I decided I had to begin—on Thanksgiving Day, as it turned out. The secretary of the institute knew this and was planning to see her family on Long Island over the holiday, so she offered her apartment to me for the days she would be gone. This would enable me to get up, walk to my office five minutes away and start work without any tramlines.[87] I moved in the day before and saw her off.

Thanksgiving morning was very quiet, all day, in fact. Everything was shut tight: shops, bookstores, of course, and libraries. I was alone, isolated, ready to write. My daughter's in-laws were appalled that I was going to miss Thanksgiving dinner with them; I took a Lean Cuisine to thaw in the Bunting microwave. I thought of a scene I wanted to write about Alice outside of her bedroom, non-events that would happen in her morphine-induced vision. Of course, I wanted to check out *Alice in Wonderland* and *Through the Looking-Glass*. I knew exactly where my Alice books were in my home library, but I was not at home. Kate and her family were already gone to visit the other side of her family. The libraries were closed. The bookstores were closed. What was I going to do? I walked to my temporary home that evening,

---

[87]   "Tramlines" are what I call external interference and distractions.

pondering my problem. I let myself into my borrowed digs and there on the kitchen table was a copy of Alice and her companion. Serendipity!

I never asked how she came to be there. I doubt my hostess would have known. I was just grateful.

The second instance also happened in Boston/Cambridge. I had finished my play about Alice James and returned home. But I went back for a directed reading of the play and started in on my next project, begun in a Radcliffe Seminar while I was at the Bunting, about journal writing, and led by a wonderful woman who became my friend and mentor, Hope Davis (1903–1993). I walked into the Schlesinger Library, the repository of what is arguably the best collection of women's documents in North America, including, of course, a treasure trove of diaries. I was wondering how to approach the research. It was like looking for several needles in a very large haystack. And there in the reading room, abandoned on a table by someone who had failed to put the book back, was an annotated bibliography of the women's diaries housed in that library. Serendipity! That is what I call being in the right place at the time. But how did that book come to be placed for me to see in the right place at the right time? I have never questioned this. I am simply grateful.

In the oil industry, a discovery well is the first successful well in a new field. The first definition of the noun "well" is a plentiful source or supply. Yes, indeed. Without epiphanies or serendipity I would dry up.

Serendipity is nice ... but I had to learn for myself that waiting isn't a life plan.

Karen Finerman (b. 1965)[88]

---

88 American businesswoman. She's worth $100m, runs a $400m hedge fund, has 2 sets of twins and 4 nannies. I guess she doesn't need serendipity.

CHAPTER SIXTEEN

BEING NICE

Do not go gentle into that good night,
Old age should burn and rave at close of day;
Rage, rage against the dying of the light.

Dylan Thomas (1914–1953)

Even as the end approaches, women find it hard to get angry. Men do it better because they have been more accustomed to asserting themselves, and they have not been punished for being outspoken. Males can be aggressive while women are just uppity (if not bitches). As they age, however, even men lose the advantage. When a chairman of the board retires, he relinquishes his authority and joins the "Honey-Do Corporation." Old joke: "Honey-Do This; Honey-Do That."

But here's an interesting finding from yet another survey.[89] People who keep on complaining as they get older actually live a little longer. This probably has something to do with self, with one's self-image, with self-righteous indignation, self-esteem,

---

[89]   *The Atlantic; Psychology Today; The New York Times; Scientic American; Forbes.*

self-defense and self- preservation, all those nice hyphenated terms I've referred to that help to define who you are and keep you going. It's not rage. At least, not the rage that Dylan Thomas had in mind, but it's not passive aggression, either. It's standing up for your self. Self again. Or maybe it really is coming of (r)age.

Life is a journey. I know I've said it before, and people long before me have been saying it for about 1500 years. It's travel in its purest form. Without going anywhere, you travel from A to Z (if you're lucky), perhaps taking notes as you go along. Don't worry, There is no written exam at the end, though there will probably be a Test. If this travel in space and time teaches you nothing else, it will tell you who you are. You will have learned whom and what you are at ease with, whom and what you are most comfortable with, and of course whom you can't stand.[90] The exasperations of the latter make some people prefer to be alone. It can be very expensive, though, single supplements being what they are.

And then there's food to be taken into account, as well as climate and comfort. Some discoveries about food you bring home with you and try to copy. I never learned how to do a proper Danish smorgasbord until I went to Denmark or a Greek salad until I went to Greece. On the other hand, I learned to bake bread at home from a step-by-step picture demonstration in the old definitive Betty Crocker cookbook (a wedding present), and *Gourmet* magazine taught me how to prepare couscous in the days before the packaged mixes.[91] So you don't have to travel to learn to cook. It's fun, though.

As for climate and comfort, I like heat but not air-conditioning. I kind of like rain, but wind makes me jumpy. I don't mind cold because I love fireplaces and it's a good excuse for a fire. This sounds as if I'm filling out a questionnaire for a compatible travel mate. Well, yes. Generally speaking, I expect to get along with

---

[90] Would you travel with you?
[91] I have a couscousière dating from those days.

people, and I do, often remaining friends with new cabinmates. Often, hoping to avoid the single supplement, I have requested a roommate on a cruise or a tour, and my prerequisite was someone who didn't smoke and didn't snore. These days, the smoking ban is automatic, and you just have to take your chances on the snoring. I had bad luck with the snoring on only one draw, but it was horrendous, a veritable Hallelujah chorus of snores rising out of one nasal passage.

Apart from the physical requirements, it's often harder to pull someone to talk to. The best assurance of that lies in the type of trip you choose. If you have opted, as I have done in the past, for a safari to East Africa, or a 10-passenger sailboat around the Galapagos Islands or an adventurous (read: cold) circumnavigation of Newfoundland, then your choice automatically guarantees travel companions with similar interests, and conversation follows. One time only I was disappointed. I was cruising down the St. Lawrence River from Toronto on a replication of a steamboat, no steam, though. I went into the dining room, as programmed, to hear the cruise director's plans for the trip and I approached a table where were already assembled a group of people, couples, 6 people in all. I asked if they minded if I joined them.

"Yes," several of them said in chorus. They minded! No singles wanted.

So I moved away and sat with a man with crutches and his 17-year-old challenged, deaf, autistic son. The father had MS and was grateful to have me climb up the tower of a fort with his son and help with the sometimes rough walking. I had determined that the boy, Robin, liked music and could feel the beat and rhythm of music through his feet, so I was certain he would agree to dance with me when I invited him for a Ladies' Choice at the dance on the Saturday night. He was happy, his dad was happy, but you should have heard the collective shocked intake of breath from the couples to see me dancing with a "retard" (their term not mine). Travel is not always broadening for people with closed minds.

The older I get, the more open my mind is, as wide as I can manage, despite my advancing age. There are programs now for keeping young(er) and exercising your mind. Workouts for the brain, often affectionately called "mental aerobics."

The program looks like fun, but there are other ways to keep stimulated and to keep learning. I've been studying Icelandic. I'm not very fluent because I don't do enough homework, but I know more than I did a couple of years ago. It's harder now.

I was 15 in my first year of university, studying Greek and Latin, and it was so easy. I could look at a page of nouns or a conjugation of a verb and get it. There were only 6 of us in the Greek class, including a veteran, older than the average age of students. This was in 1946, right after World War Two, when the populations of the universities burgeoned with returning soldiers. When I celebrated my 16th birthday, he warned me: now that I was that old, it would be all downhill, and I would never be able to learn my verbs so quickly again. I thought of that a lot when I struggled with Icelandic. Too soon old, too late smart, and so little time—but there's always enough time to be nice. I'll get to it.

Elise Boulding (1920–2010) was a Quaker sociologist, a teacher at Dartmouth, wife of the economist Kenneth Boulding, mother of five children and a feminist. Her work reassured me that I had, if not the world at my fingertips, at least a broad spectrum of it. She used the word nurturance,[92] emphasizing the need of it for adults as well as for children, and the responsibility of men as well as women to provide it. She shared this view with a contemporary feminist, Dorothy Dinnerstein (1923–1992), whose influential book *The Mermaid and the Minotaur* (1976) you will find in every feminist bibliography published around that time. Boulding's

---

[92] "Emotional and physical nourishment and care given to someone," not only children. Caregivers, take note.

book *The Underside of History: A View of Women through Time* (1976) examined the changing, yet unchanging, roles of women throughout history. In all, she published 11 books. I own *The Underside of History,* but I found a little booklet, hardly more than a brochure, that had the most lasting effect on me. It's a copy of a speech she gave to the Vanier Institute of the Family at a meeting in Banff in 1981. My little copy is lined and highlighted, and I learn from it every time I re-read it.

The most arresting thought to me was her idea of the 200-year-present, more applicable today even than when she wrote it because so many more people are living so long. It's a simple idea: A child born today has a potential life span of 100 years. There are people living today who have been alive for almost 100 years or more. Thus, within a person's lifetime, one can be in touch with a living present of 200 years. This is without recourse to history books but open to living memory forward or backward. It has powerful repercussions, past, present and future. Today, this idea is referred to as "The Long Now," and it's comforting because things remain familiar for a while, and allow time for us to change and to adjust to change. The Long Now, with its overview of history, puts things into perspective and makes it possible to relax.

Some travellers in time, who don't take this long view, still tend to get irritated. They get annoyed in other countries because they're not like home. In *The Accidental Tourist* (first published 1981), a novel by Anne Tyler, the hero, Macon Leary, is a professional traveller who makes his living seeking out and reporting on familiar oases in foreign lands where tourists can feel right at home, almost as if they had never left.

In my Other Life, Bill and the Stratford Festival producer went to England on theatre business and took their wives. So the other wife and I went to have our hair done at a posh place on Bond Street. I have always let a new hairdresser have his head—mine, I mean. How are you going to learn something new? It's only hair, and the good thing is it will grow out. So I sat quietly, waiting for the results. My companion, on the other hand, gave her guy detailed instructions on how to do her hair, to get it right, the way she had it done at home. When we were done, I think we both looked pretty good, but when our husbands complimented us, she said, "Oh, but it's just like home. I needn't have bothered." She hadn't changed. I was nice; I didn't say anything.

Irritation is in the eye of the irritated.[93] I'm nice. I try to be nice. As a matter of fact, it's one of my problems in my life journey, as it is for a lot of women, especially for women my age or close to it. Perhaps it's too late to change, but I am trying to stop being so nice. It's hard to quit because it is so ingrained (or hard-wired?).

I've dropped hints of it already; for example, my inability to say no to my father when he wanted me to learn to touch-type.[94] He was old school, mind you. When I was still at home in my late teens, I was not allowed to go downtown in mid-July without stockings and gloves. I thought of that when I was in Mexico a few years ago. The temperature in Mexico City was 40 degrees Celsius and the women in the streets were glowing in their girdles and stockings.[95] That makes me think of Playtex girdles. The only thing that lay between you and mid-summer torture was a dusting of talcum powder. I lived through my formative years in such man-made prisons. Female students at universities in my day wore skirts, absolutely no pants/slacks/trousers, whatever. Jeans were unheard of. Women travellers today still have to be careful about their dress in some countries. Men still make the prisons.

As with the clothes, so with other restrictions in deportment and behaviour: respect, whether deserved or not, was to be accorded to one's elders and one's superiors. Define superior. Girls, especially, were not supposed—allowed—to argue or disagree.

---

[93] Or maybe it's a mote.

[94] He was right, of course.

[95] Remember that line: "Horses sweat, men perspire and women glow"?

They were expected to be agreeable and polite and affable—in short, to be nice.

I wrote a poem about this in the introduction to my book of poetic monologues based on the diaries of women,[96] and I'll quote a few lines.[97]

This is from the section entitled "The New Rules;" they were the rigid rules that were handed down like gospel to the women of my and later generations:

> Thou shalt remember to be nice,
> Bearing in mind the good advice
> Of grandmother:
> You catch more flies with honey than
> With vinegar (for every man
> Wants his mother).
>
> Thou shalt love, honour and obey,
> Not only on your wedding day,
> But all your life.
> No one gave you any choice;
> You're expected to rejoice
> To be a wife.
>
> Thou shalt always shut your eyes
> To nasty facts and compromise
> Your deepest feeling
> Always smiling through your tears
> Never letting on your fears—
> They're too revealing.

---

96   *The Better Half: Women's Voices,* Black Moss Press, 1995.
97   I have given myself copyright permission. Fair usage.

Toronto psychologist Dr. Evelyn Sommers has published a book about niceness. *The Tyranny of Niceness: Unmasking the Need for Approval* (2005) encourages women to challenge the demand for their silence and obedience. To younger women, this may seem like a given. To female boomers, especially those nearing retirement, especially those who find themselves the flattened filling in the so-called Sandwich Generation, the tyranny exists and still intimidates them. They are trying to learn to live without guilt, which isn't easy, but then it's not easy to live with it, either.

I can't argue with it; I'm halfway between then and now. The older I get, though, the more uncharted is the territory I'm moving into. I'm freer now than I was even 20 years ago[98] to make my own decisions. Fewer people have made them because not many have lived this long, nor been articulate about it.

I have found it interesting to note the comments people have made about aging. Well-known, famous people, who are not afraid of saying what they think, have differing attitudes to their condition. For example:

- Philip Roth said old age is a massacre
- Oliver Saks said it's a joy
- May Sarton said it was an ascent
- Maurice Chevalier said it was not so bad when you consider the alternative
- "Old age is not for sissies"— attributed to Bette Davis but said by others, including my aunt Phyllis
- "Old age, believe me, is a good and pleasant thing." Confucius
- Ralph Waldo Emerson said all diseases run into one— old age.
- "We're on the verge of breaking through this definition of age as leprosy." Betty Friedan

---

[98]   Try 46. I was widowed in 1973.

- "Life is more stress-free, you have more control over your time, *you no longer have to please others* and you have the power to speak the truth." Lindsay Green[99]
- "If you are so worried that you have to cut your face up to make yourself happier, you're with the wrong guy." Jerry Hall[100]

And I say old age is not a disease; it's a journey. You may have noticed that I found an equal number of women with something to say about old age. It took a search. I noticed that they were less belligerent about growing old, for the most part expressing resignation rather than anger. Or maybe it's because we have become truly invisible, also inaudible. In any case, we are all preparing, each in our own way, to head for the departure lounge with a bang or a whimper, but not, it seems, with rage.

I have nothing to declare but my genius.

attributed to Oscar Wilde

---

[99] Author of the book, *You Could Live a Long time: Are You Ready?* (2010). Note what she says about pleasing others. (Italics mine.)
[100] Jerry Hall had a long-term (1977–1999) common-law marriage to rock star Mick Jagger. She sounds independent, at least being unwilling to cut her face up.

CHAPTER SEVENTEEN

LEAVING

**I'm not afraid of dying. I just don't
want to be there when it happens.**

Woody Allen (b. 1935)

You who are so young, tell me, when was the last time you did
something for the last time? Unless it was something momentous,
requiring an act of will and a statement of intent, like giving up
cigarettes or booze or a lover, it's possible you don't know. Not that
you don't remember; you simply don't know. Life is still long, and
time stretches like an endless tennis court or swimming pool or ski
trail ahead of you. Often you won't know until years later that the
last time was the last time. I didn't. I still don't—not everything.[101]

Take bowling. When was the last time you bowled? Unless
you're in a league and bowling is your life, you may have trouble
recalling. The last time I bowled, as it turned out, had a memory
tag attached to it. It was in my Other Life; our family was intact;
my then living husband and I took all four children bowling one

---

[101] I mean, will I ever eat snails again?

Saturday afternoon in Stratford where we lived. The phone was ringing as we came in the door. I answered.

"Do you bowl?" said a breathy voice.

"As a matter of fact, we just finished bowling," I said, thinking it was a survey. Not as many in those days, but still.

"Who? Who bowls?"

"The whole family," I said. "Who is this?" I'm good at voices, but I hadn't recognized this one.

"I mean, do you *bowl*?" he insisted.

"Oh," I said. "Oh. Oh." His pronunciation had finally caught up with me, and I understood what he was trying to say. Ball!

"You're being lewd," I said, and hung up.

The kids laughed at me, but anyone would have been misled by the man's poor enunciation. Anyway, that's how I remember the last time I bowled.

We are not often given such a mnemonic to help us remember a milestone. Often we have passed a turning-point in our lives so smoothly, without anything to mark it as a turning-point, and so moderately, just a gradual shift in direction that we don't notice till after our momentum has taken us a long way past, too late to acknowledge.

Even menopause. The adjustments and changes are gradual and never seem definitive. I mean, it's not like rain stopping and the sun coming out. There is no one day that I can look back on and say, "That's the day I became a crone." Not like the first menses. Most women can remember that clearly. I suppose a man will never forget the first time he shaved. Is that true? Maybe not. From my observation, whiskers are incremental and only gradually require a full frontal daily attack. Still, firsts are easier to pinpoint than lasts.

I remember the day my father, who was dying of cancer at home for as long as he and my mother could manage, crept back to bed and said, "That is the last time I will shave myself at the bathroom mirror." He knew, and honoured the knowledge with formal recognition. Later, I used that recognition in the play I wrote about the old woman in a room.[102]

Her light bulb burns out, and she painfully replaces it, standing precariously on a chair and reaching up in the dark. Safely returned to the floor, she looks up and says, "That is the last time I will change a light bulb."

Most last times slip away like a suspension rather than a cessation of activity. Weather, a bad ankle, loss of a partner or lack of money, any or all might cause someone to stop playing tennis or making love without noticing that the last time was the very last time. And sometimes you get fooled, and just when you think you've done something for the last time, something comes up. Like changing diapers.

That's another thing that changes (pun!) slowly. Children don't abandon diapers all at once or altogether. Even after a child is daytime toilet-trained, special occasions, like a long car trip or an exciting party or a sudden illness, can justify the temporary use of diapers, and night training takes a little longer. In my day, before disposables, with four children to see through this first milestone, I had a full diaper pail, so to speak, for 10 years. That's when I first put into words my hard-won philosophy: "Now isn't forever; it only feels like it." Then there was a reprise.

I had grandchildren and had to learn all over again. Diapers tucked and folded differently than they used to, and sticky tape made safety pins almost obsolete. Now, they have sticky wraps and pull-ups, don't they? Anyway, I got to diaper again. By now I think it's certain that the last grandchild has been born. (Emily is in her twenties.) So I likely won't have any more diapers to change, and I can hang my memories out to dry. I doubt anyone will trust me to diaper a great grandchild, should I live so long.

In the generation between babies, I pinned a diaper once. Back in our theatre days when my husband was the manager and I the

---

102   *A Place on Earth,* 1982.

unpaid groupie chatelaine of the Stratford Festival Theatre, John Hirsch (1930-1989) masterminded a musical called *Satyricon, 1969,* adapted from *Petronius* by Tom Hendry (1929–2012), involving not only the Festival company but also a stand-up vaudeville comedian, a juggler, a tall white stripper and three black singers, all imported from New York. We had a backyard pool party for the cast and crew. One of the singers came late when the party was in full swing. She searched me out in the crowd of about 75 people.

"Do you diaper?" she asked me.

"As in people? I suppose it's like riding a bicycle," I said.

She handed me a small triangle of orange cotton and one big safety pin. I took her to a bedroom and she stripped and lay down on the bed with her head on my right. I made her turn the other way, as I can diaper in only one direction. Not a bad job, I was thinking as I finished. Then she made her next request: eyelash adhesive. In those days, I had some, and she used it to glue on two small orange-sequined pasties to match her diaper before she went out to get a tan. I am happy to report that she did not attempt to swim. (The glue was not waterproof.) That would have been a memorable occasion for my last diapering, but I had grandchildren after that. So you never know. It ain't over till it's over.

God knows when it will be over, and He hasn't told me yet. It's not as if I'm sitting in the departure lounge, waiting for the boarding announcement. Very few people have it as simple as that.

So my travelling days may not be over. I can't reminisce about that far country, still far, still unknown. I'm not in any hurry, not yet. I do have a few questions.

I have a favourite *Peanuts* strip from the comic series by Charles M. Schulz (1922–2000). His hero, Charlie Brown, is sitting in the dark on the 4th of July, waiting for the sun to come up.

"Life sure is strange," he says.

"And they say we only come this way once."

Last frame: "What did I come this way for?"

That's one of the questions.

I have a few more.

In an appraisal of *I Am a Strange Loop* (2007) by Douglas R. Hofstadter,[103] the reviewer, another polymath, Uriah Kriegel, brings up three questions. Kriegel doesn't make it clear if the questions are his or Hofstadter's, but here they are, challenging our understanding of the world:

1) Why is there something rather than nothing?
2) Why is some of what there is alive?
3) Why is some of what is alive conscious, or self-aware?

As I arrive at the launching pad, it is with temerity that I try to link my thoughts with those of these two philosophical scientific giants but I, too, am a strange loop; that is, I am self-referential, and if you didn't know that by now, you haven't been paying attention. I'm also dragging in Charlie Brown and Julian Jaynes to help me think about the final journey.

Charlie Brown you already know. Julian Jaynes (1922–2000) was an American psychologist, best known for his book *The Origin of Consciousness in the Breakdown of the Bicameral Mind* (1976 and 2000). His idea that the ancient peoples were not conscious influenced my thinking about the development of the self, that is, the consciousness of self.

Which brings me to my present conundrum. It's difficult to deal with one's own crossing because it's hard to contemplate non-awareness; that is, the loss of self. That's probably why it's so tough to come to terms with the thought of Alzheimer's, involving the

---

[103] Douglas Richard Hofstadter is an American professor of cognitive science whose research focuses on the sense of "I", consciousness, analogy-making, artistic creation, literary translation, and discovery in mathematics and physics. *Wikipedia.*

loss of self-awareness or consciousness. And that's why I'm stopping at the boarding gate. I'm not the only one. Other travellers have stopped here, waiting for a different means of passage, but with the same destination, more or less.

Little as most people these days know of Greek mythology, the image of the river Styx sticks. The river marked the boundary between Earth and the Underworld, or Hell, in Christian terms. The ferryman who plied the boat necessary to cross the river was called Charon. Woody Allen uses the image of the boat in his movie *Scoop (2007)*; it has a full load of souls, a captive audience for the card tricks Allen's character performs. Potential passengers seem to have no trouble recognizing the image of the boat. They're just not ready to book the crossing. This, after all, is the last big one. Who knows what's on the other side? Ay, there's the rub.

Well, I'm not going there, not today. I have to think about it some more. I don't mean I'm not ever going there. I'm not making an absurd bid for immortality. But right now, in my present state of health, vitality and mental alertness, I think I can carry on for a little while longer, albeit a little more slowly. As we know, anything can happen. My current, admirable habits of good nutrition and exercise are not efforts to prolong my life but simply practical means of enjoying the life I have left. So when I say I'm not going there I just mean I'm not going there today. Tomorrow, maybe.

... and our little life is rounded with a sleep.

William Shakespeare (1564–1616), *The Tempest*

THIS WOMAN, OLDER

Well, I still get tired, even more so than before, but I try to allow for a longer recovery time than I used to need.

Does anyone remember "all-nighters"? I looked it up, and it's in the online dictionary: "an event or task that sometimes lasts all night, especially before a study session or examination—a feat performed by overworked students and physicians"—like my granddaughter, the doctor. Long after my overworked student days, when I was in the throes of rehearsing a new play and needed rewrites for the next day, I didn't stay up all night. I went to bed and woke at 4 a.m. to write. I had discovered that I kept on writing in my head while I slept and thus solved a lot of my problems. I began to be aware of the wisdom that comes with experience and age. My body betrays me more often now but not—so far—my brain. It's still there when I need it, thank goodness.

A while ago, I tripped over a manhole cover on Bloor Street and fell full-length-forward but not face-forward. I turned my head so that the sidewalk missed my eyes, nose and teeth. I fell onto my knees and forearms; my right arm took the full impact. Shaken and aching overnight in spite of an ice pack and even a (rare) painkiller, I forced my son to drop me at a hospital emergency room to check my bones. The doctor who examined my X-rays looked at my chart and asked,

"How did you get to be 87 years old and all you have is sciatica?" (I never mention osteoporosis.)

My answer: Ancestors and swimming.

Even so, I'm catching up and beginning to pass my ancestors in terms of age. My mother died at 82; her older sister at 97 and their father, my grandfather, in his 90s. I was 83 when I wrote the first draft of *This Old Woman*, a tribute to and rebuttal of Roger Angell's *New Yorker* essay (March 2015). I'm 87 as I write this, and I'll be 88 when it's published so now I am officially old-old (see page 24). Stats Canada stopped counting at 85. Most people do. The point is I have few role models, no close precedents to give me hints of what to expect or how I should conduct myself, or when the time is up.

I have noted my loss of family and furniture and doctors and compared myself to a duck in a shooting gallery, but the mounting losses are painful. Contemporary friends, my peer group, have all but disappeared. Several years ago, I wrote in my Christmas letter that the main reason I write and read seasonal greetings and don't dare to stop is that it's the only way to announce my continuing presence on Earth.[104] I write, therefore I am.

Too often I have sent a card to have it responded to by a bereaved wife or sister or daughter (men don't usually bother) 3 to 6 months after the season, and who knows how long after the departure?[105] Unless the person was famous, obituaries are local. I've been making my own sad independent discoveries as well when I realize I haven't heard from an old friend for quite a while and I Google a name (in another city) to find an unexpected obituary. I dread it now, so I've stopped searching. Instead, I cherish past memories.

---

[104] A daily (regular) blog is another way now, but others have to read it.
[105] I hate the term "passed" but others don't like "died."

No one mentions the painful part of travel: losing new friends. Of course, I know I can't expect every compatible traveller to keep up with former ship-mates—ships that pass in the night. As the sun pulls away from the shore, so the easy daily friendships sink into the west, aka oblivion. And some of those people die, too, and I'll never know. I met one new charming friend early on who had travelled much more than I had and who was much more realistic about our brief connection. We said our farewells and before I could make any promises about keeping in touch, she said, "You were a good companion on this trip. I'll remember you."

In the end, memory is all most of us have, and we're lucky to have that. Other friends, no longer geographically or physically close and sometimes even if they are, slip into our past and fade away. I can't blame them or myself for that. One loses the currency of friendship. I acknowledged that when my husband died. I was no longer a wife, and I had very little left in common with friends and neighbours. I'm sure this happens to older widows, too, but my gap widened because suddenly I was trying to make a living, and I was the one who had less time for casual companionship.

Others, too, have left, though not physically. My older contemporary friends—those who are still living—are not as conversant with computers as I am, though my children and grandchildren shake their heads at my technological ineptitude. I can understand not hearing from them, computer illiterate as they are—my friends, not my grandchildren. Other old friends just don't like writing, the physical act of writing: their stiff, non-compliant fingers and the time-consuming business of assembling paper, pen and stamps and then the trouble of finding a post office or a mailbox.

I have a theory about mailboxes. Long ago, I read a science fiction story (this was before I noticed writers, so I can't tell you who wrote it). An inventor discovers a means of getting rid of metal waste, like razor blades and cars. He drops a used razor blade into a box he has created and it disappears. Totally. (It was probably a tesseract.) The man becomes an instant hero because he has solved a major landfill problem. Cut to a dying planet where the living creatures have run out of food, with nothing left for them to sustain life. Suddenly, a razor blade drops out of nowhere and bounces onto the barren surface, followed very soon by a veritable deluge of metal nourishment all the critters will ever need to keep on living. Happy ending. See? I figure these drop boxes have been placed all over our known world. They look exactly like mail boxes. This explains why people never answer their mail: it's going to another planet.

Email doesn't have to be sent to another planet to disappear. It's much easier to dispose of. When it first burst into our consciousness, it was such fun. One replied to everything, even spam. No one bothers any more. No one answers mail, not to say "please, thank you, not interested," or "too busy." People used to press *reply*, *return*, or *send*. Not necessary. No response means *NO*. It must be so much easier not to burden a secretary with this duty, easier simply not to press the key and thus avoid the polite platitudes and negatives altogether.

I know I am not being amusing. This is not funny. If I sound a bit tetchy, well, I am. But I'm still nice. I keep remembering what Thumper told Bambi,[106] repeating his mother's advice:

"If you can't say somethin' nice, don't say nothin' at all."

Yet another survey tells us that elderly people are happier than middle-aged ones. Well, yes, and there's a lot to be happy about. One reason to be happy, as I've said before, is that I'm still here—still here, for example, to meet my new great-grandchildren.

I had trouble finding a publisher for this book. I've listed some of my losses already: family and friends, doctors and dentists, also publishers, editors, producers, agents and publicists; in short, the contacts I needed—still need—to pursue my career. The pursuit

---

[106] *Bambi* is a 1942 animated Disney film, based on the book *Bambi, A Life in the Woods* by Austrian author Felix Salten (1869-1949).

has become a rabbit chase. Most, if not all, of my contacts are retired, dead or gaga. The few who remain don't remember me. The new ones I have found don't want to. I am old, you see. I've had trouble reconciling this lack of recognition with my track record and list of publications and productions. It's who I used to be.

I had to search for a platform where I could be found again. A comeback? Young advisors recommended Facebook. I tried it. I didn't befriend easily. I mean, why should I be friends with people I don't know and know nothing about—nor they with me? Nor do I want to presume friendship with someone whose name I know (famous) or whom I have met briefly. I was pleased to come across a few people from my past who haven't died. And I was interested to see what relatives by marriage, mostly cousins, are doing with their lives. But Facebook is not going to provide the readers I need for my book. They are not my audience.

Mind you, Facebook is charming and beguiling and distracting—and incredibly time-consuming. My fault. I didn't realize what was happening until it was almost too late. I don't really need a "life-changing shock or surprise of my life" daily. I don't really want to know what child actors look like now, or how lovely formerly young women look now with face-lifts gone awry. I don't need to know what so-and-so is really worth, especially after I looked up me and laughed out loud. Tell my bank manager that. Spare me the knowledge of actors' IQs. I can live without knowing the names of their pets. You've seen one Grumpy Cat, you've seen them all. I could go on and on, and Facebook does. I've had enough. It took my computer-literate grandson to get me off of Facebook. He had to say no, no, NO! to different offers and ploys to keep me in the fold. I'm gone. No Facebook, no Twitter, no Instagram, no Pinterest, no Links. Is that everything? I really am on my way to being a neo-Luddite.

More surveys reveal that older people are happier than middle-aged people, matching in life satisfaction that of the younger generation. I think it's *almost* true. Perhaps I wouldn't say happy. Maybe content. Not complaining. The Long Now gave me some perspective, as I have pointed out, although Right-Now has rather suddenly and unexpectedly become quite stressful.

Apparently a U-shaped bend appeared on the happiness scale: The bottom of the U shows up at about age 48, just when children and aging parents are their most demanding and expensive and job pressures are the most stressful. We happy old-timers prize health, security and family above fame and riches, although these prizes do involve money. Ah, well. As Joe E. Lewis said, "I don't like money, actually, but it quiets the nerves."[107]

You may have noticed I quote a lot of people. I find it comforting, and I still have a good memory. So the following sounds less final than my conclusion to chapter 17. Who knows? I might be back. I'm still writing.

I grow old ... I grow old ...

T. S. Eliot, *The Love Song of J. Alfred Prufrock*

---

[107] Joe E. Lewis, singer, comedian (1902–1971). Frank Sinatra played him in the movie *The Joker is Wild*. 1957.

THE TAO OF TRAVEL

The last section of Paul Theroux's book *The Tao of Travel* offers 10 suggestions to follow when you travel. I don't agree with all of them, but there are a few I like:

- Leave home (well, duh)
- Go alone
- Travel light
- Keep a journal
- Read a novel that has no relation to the place you're in
- Make a friend

You, of course, can make your own list.

Here's mine:

WYLIE'S BASIC RULES OF TRAVEL

1. I am waterproof. This doesn't mean that I don't get wet; it means that I don't mind if I do.
2. I never get constipated. (This is a rule that I imposed.)
3. I can sleep anywhere, and if I can't, I make use of the time.
4. I take socks and a sweater wherever I go.

5. I always forget my pills, so it's better not to have any to take.
6. I always remember pen and paper.
7. I take my smile with me.
8. I bounce pretty well, and bend, but I do not break (well, not often).
9. I can eat anything, and if I can't, I don't make a fuss about it, especially when it won't do any good.
10. My mouth is open.
11. So is my mind.
12. Never say no—within reason!

RULES FOR TRAVEL BY MORITZ THOMSEN

1. Dollar meals if I can find them
2. Five dollar hotels, if they still exist
3. No guided tours
4. No visits to historical monuments or old churches
5. No mixed drinks in fancy bars
6. No hanging around places where English might be spoken

Moritz Thomsen (1915–1991) was a Peace Corps volunteer. His books have been praised by writers such as Paul Theroux and Larry McMurtry. *Wikipedia.*

TWO SIMPLE RULES FROM JAN MORRIS

1. One is E.M. Forster's guide to Alexandria: "The best way to know Alexandria is to wonder aimlessly."
2. The second is from the Psalms: "Grin like a dog and run about through the city."

(In other words, aimlessly.)

And don't forget, rules are made to be broken, or at least to be bent a little.

SEVENTEETH CENTURY NUN'S PRAYER

Lord, thou knowest better than I know myself that I am growing older and will some day be old. Keep me from the fatal habit of thinking I must say something on every subject and on every occasion. Release me from craving to straighten out everybody's affairs. Make me thoughtful but not moody; helpful but not bossy. With my vast store of wisdom it seems a pity not to use it all, but Thou knowest Lord, that I want a few friends at the end.

Keep my mind free from the recital of endless details; give me wings to get to the point. Seal my lips on my aches and pains. They are increasing and love of rehearsing them is becoming sweeter as the years go by. I dare not ask for grace enough to enjoy the tales of other's pains, but help me to endure them with patience. I dare not ask for improved memory, but for a growing humility and a lessening cocksureness when my memory seems to clash with the memories of others. Teach me the glorious lesson that occasionally I may be mistaken.

Keep me reasonably sweet; I do not want to be a saint—some of them are so hard to live with—but a sour old person is one of the crowning works of the Devil. Give me the ability to see good things in unexpected places and talents in unexpected people. And, give me, O Lord, the grace to tell them so.

Amen

There is some doubt whether this is authentic

If you like it, it doesn't matter, does it? The following is authentic.

RESOLUTIONS WHEN I COME TO BE OLD
by Jonathan Swift (1667–1745)

Not to

Marry a young Woman.

Keep young Company unless they really desire it.

Be peevish or morose, or suspicious.

Scorn present Ways, or Wits, or Fashions, or Men, or War, etc.

Be fond of Children, or let them come near me hardly.

Tell the same Story over and over to the same People.

Be covetous.

Neglect decency, or cleanliness, for fear of falling into Nastiness.

Be over severe with young People, but give Allowances for their youthfull follies, and Weaknesses.

Be influenced by, or give ear to knavish tattling Servants, or others.

Be too free of advise (sic) nor trouble any but those that desire it.

Desire some good Friends to inform me which of these Resolutions I break, or neglect, & wherein; and reform accordingly.

Talk much, nor of my self.

Boast of my former beauty, or strength, or favour with Ladies, etc.

Hearken to Flatteries, nor conceive I can be beloved by a young woman. et eos qui hereditatem captant odisse ac vitare. (and them who shall be heirs to evade and avoid to hate.)

Be positive or opinionated.

Sett up for observing all these Rules, for fear I should observe none.

BIBLIOGRAPHY for *ENDINGS*

Alexander, Jo, et al., editors. *Women and Aging: An Anthology by Women.* Calyx Books, 1986.

Améry, Jean. *On Aging: Revolt and Resignation*, translated by John D. Barlow.
Indiana University Press, 1994.

Barnes, Julian, *nothing to be frightened of*, Random House, 2008.

Bird, Isabella. *A Lady's Life in the Rocky Mountains.* 1879.

Bond, Edward. *The Sea* (a play). Originally produced 1973.

Calisher, Hortense. *Age.* Weidenfeld & Nicholson, 1987.

Capponi, Pat. *Upstairs in the Crazy House, The Life of a Psychiatric Survivor.* Penguin, 1992.

Cole, Thomas R., and Mary G. Winkler, editors. *The Oxford Book of Aging: Reflections on the Journey of Life.* Oxford University Press, 1994.

Comfort, Alex. *A Good Age.* Simon and Shuster, 1976.

Crone magazine, established 2008, the successor to *Crone Chronicles* which ended publication in 2001.

Cruikshank, Margaret. *Learning to be Old: Gender, Culture, and Aging.* Rowman & Littlefield Publishers Inc., 2003.

Csikszentmihalyi, Mihaly. *Flow: The Psychology of Optimal Experience.* Harper Row, 2009.

Daly, Mary. *Webster's First New Intergalactic Wickedary of the English Language,* (with Jane Caputi and Sudie Rakusin). Beacon Press, 1987.

Dickson, Paul. *The Official Explanations.* Delacorte Press, 1980.

Doidge, Norman, M.D. *The Brain that Changes Itself,* 2007, and *The Brain's Way of Healing,* 2015.

Dossey, Larry, M.D. *Be Careful What You Pray For. Harper One,* 1997.

Erikson, Eric, *Childhood and Society,* W.W. Norton and Company, 1966
Identity: Youth and Crisis, W.W. Norton and Company, 1968

Frankl, Viktor E. *Man's Search for Meaning.* Simon and Schuster 1959.

Fussell, Paul. *Abroad.* Oxford University Press, 1980.

Genova, Lisa. *Still Alice.* (Self-published) iUniverse Press, 2007; Pocket Books, 2009.

Gibran, Kahlil. *The Prophet.* Alfred A. Knopf, 1923.

Hitchens, Christopher. *Mortality.* McLelland & Stewart, 2012.

Huxley, Aldous. *Crome Yellow*, 1921; *Those Barren Leaves,* 1925; *Point Counterpoint*, 1928.

Iyer, Pico. *The Art of Stillness, Adventures in Going Nowhere.* Simon and Schuster, 2014. (Note an earlier essay, "The Joy of Quiet").

Judt, Tony. *The Memory Chalet.* Penguin Books, 2010.

Kesey, Ken. *One Flew Over the Cuckoo's Nest.* Viking Press & Signet Books, 1962.

Kingsley, Mary. *Travels in West Africa.* 1897, Folio Edition, 2014.

Kinsley, Michael. *Old Age, A Beginner's Guide.* Tim Duggan Books, 2016.

Klein, Daniel. *Travels with Epicurus: A Journey to a Greek Island in Search of a Fulfilled Life.* Penguin Books, 2012.

Klinenberg, Eric. *Going Solo: The Extraordinary Rise and Surprising Appeal of Living Alone.* Penguin Press, 2012.

Lively, Penelope. *Dancing Fish and Ammonites: A Memoir.* Viking, 2013.

Macdonald, Barbara, with Cynthia Rich. *Look Me in the Eye: Old Women, Aging and Ageism.* Spinsters, Ink, 1983.

Martz, Sandra, editor. *When I am an Old Woman I Shall Wear Purple: An Anthology of Short Stories and Poetry.* Papier-Maché Press, 1987.

Maslow, Abraham H. *Toward a Psychology of Being.* Van Nostrand, 1968.

Mednick, Sara C. *Take a Nap! Change Your Life*. Workman Publishing, 2006.

Morris, Mary, *Nothing to Declare: Memories of a Woman Travelling Alone, Paladin Books, 1988*

Murphy, Dervla. *Full Tilt: Ireland to India With a Bicycle*. The Overlook Press, 1987 (originally published in 1965).

Pollan, Michael. *The Omnivore's Dilemma*, Penguin Press, 2006; *Food Rules: An Eater's Manual*. Penguin Press, 2008.

Rybcynski, Witold. *Home: A Short History of an Idea*. Penguin, 1987.

Sand, George. *The Intimate Journal*. Translated and edited by Marie Jennie Howe, Academy Chicago Publishers, 1984.

Dr. Seuss: Theodore Seuss Giesel, Oh, the Places You'll Go! Random House, first published 1990, the last book published in his lifetime.

Stark, Freya (1893-1993). *The Southern Gates of Arabia: A Journey in the Hadhramaut*, 1936. Folio Edition, 2014.

Stock, Gregory. *The Book of Questions*. Workman Publishing, 1987 (revised, 2013).

Storr, Anthony. *Solitude: A Return to the Self,* originally published 1988.Theroux, Paul, ed. *The Tao of Travel: Enlightenments from Lives on the Road,* Houghton Mifflin Harcourt, 2011.

Summers, Evelyn, *The Tyranny of Niceness: Unmasking the Need for Approval, Dundurn Press, 2005*

Thomsen, Moritz, Living Poor: A Peace Corps Chronicle, University of Washington Press, 1969

Toffler, Alvin. *Future Shock.* Random House, 1970.

Tyler, Anne. *The Accidental Tourist.* Grassroots Press, 2017.

Vidal, Gore. *Palimpsest: A Memoir.* Penguin, 1996.

Wikipedia. 2018. "Conspicuous Consumption." Last edited 18 March 2019. https://en.wikipedia.org/wiki/Conspicuous_consumption

———. 2018. "Douglas Richard Hofstadter." Last edited 14 April 2019. https://en.wikipedia.org/wiki/Douglas_Hofstadter

———. 2018. "Hylomorphism." Last edited 7 April 2019. https://en.wikipedia.org/wiki/Hylomorphism

———. 2018. "Midden." Last edited 17 April 2019. https://en.wikipedia.org/wiki/Midden

Author illustration © Heather Spears

Betty Jane Wylie is a distinguished non-fiction author and playwright, whose work also includes poetry and librettos. With over thirty-five books and three dozen plays to her credit--published by a wide range of presses--she has written bestsellers such as *Beginnings: A Book for Widows*, memoirs, self-help studies, belles lettres accounts of women diarists and also of her own Icelandic background, a book about financial planning and even several cookbooks. She received an Order of Canada in 2003 and has been a writer-in-residence at libraries across the country, Chair of the Canadian Writers Union, and a Fellow of The Bunting Institute at Radcliffe Harvard. A graduate of the University of Manitoba, which granted her an honorary doctorate and collects her literary papers, she says she is very old, but who knows?

Betty Jane Wylie's Endings is not to be taken lightly, though its tone is deceptively light and its style lively and conversational. She extracts interesting anecdotes and observations from her long, well-lived life and asks serious questions: How do we live as old people? As old women? What can we expect? How do we handle the time that is left? Eighty-eight year old Wylie tackles these subjects thoughtfully, but also with humour and charm. You won't just enjoy this book; if you're approaching this stage of life, you will find it both salutary and richly entertaining. Endings is a valuable contribution to the literature about and by aging people.

- Sharon Butala

Three times short-listed for the Governor-General's award, she published her latest book, Season of Fury and Wonder, in May, 2019.

"While demographic studies tell of our aging population, most people--and governments–barely acknowledge this shift. Shortly before his death in 43 B.C., the Roman writer Cicero meditated on old age in De Senectute, a classic recently translated as How to Grow Old. This challenging subject now occupies many contemporary writers in their so-called 'golden years', with popular new memoirs from Diana Athill, Donald Hall and Roger Angel offering intimate accounts of their dilemmas and solutions. In Endings: A Book for Almost Everyone, Betty Jane Wylie, the Canadian non-fiction writer, playwright and blogger, adds her warm-hearted but wry voice to an important growing genre. Admirers of Wylie's work will recognize her compassionate approach to life's struggles, while readers new to her will enjoy the frank, hard-won wisdom of a woman who looks at life clear-eyed. Old age, she tells us, takes 'guts and grace', which is also a good description of this memoir.

–Richard Teleky, Professor of Humanities at York University and author of Ordinary Paradise: Essays on Art and Culture

CPSIA information can be obtained
at www.ICGtesting.com
Printed in the USA
LVHW100822271019
635460LV00001B/1/P